Interior of Residence for Ashbel Green Englewood. N.J.

Bruce Price Arch't. N.Y.

View in Stair Hall.

· Main Hall · · Library · · Drawing · R'm ·

Late Victorian Interiors

and Interior Details

WILLIAM B. TUTHILL

DOVER PUBLICATIONS, INC.
MINEOLA, NEW YORK

Bibliographical Note

This Dover edition, first published in 2010, is an unabridged republication of *Interiors and Interior Details: Fifty-Two Large Quarto Plates,* originally published by William T. Comstock, New York, in 1882. Please note that the plates have been reproduced at 90% of their original size.

Library of Congress Cataloging-in-Publication Data

Tuthill, William Burnet, 1855–1929.
  [Interiors and interior details]
  Late Victorian interiors and interior details / William B. Tuthill. — Dover ed.
    p. cm.
  Originally published: Interiors and interior details. New York : William T. Comstock, 1882.
    ISBN-13: 978-0-486-47603-2
    ISBN-10: 0-486-47603-0
    1. Interior architecture. 2. Architecture—Details. I. Title.

NA2851.T9 2010
729—dc22

                                                                    2010020989

Manufactured in the United States by LSC Communications
47603005   2017
www.doverpublications.com

INTRODUCTION

———— •·• ————

IT HAS become almost a rule, in the erection of our dwellings, for the interior treatment to claim a preponderating part of the attention and thought which is given to the work.

An artistic taste, more or less developed, a very general desire to have those things about us which indicate a cultured refinement, together with a possibly laudable emulation, has given us multitudes of designs, beautiful, unique and original.

Most of these have, in the first instance, been the production of cultivated artists. While their leading has been well followed by a numerous class of fairly-equipped designers, who have given to their work, in many cases, an unusual amount of study, the results have not been artistically what they might have been. Many of the designs are crude in conception and feeble in execution. Details are studied to the neglect of the design ; originality is sought for its own sake, and too often becomes extreme.

The successful design of interiors has different conditions than those applicable to exterior work. There are no sharply defined shadows, no extreme high lights—the strong elements of a design which is to be seen in sunlight. There is but a diffused and indirect light, in which each and every member has its part of the general effect to bear. That which for exterior work might be accomplished by a bold, sharp line of shadow, must here be treated as a distinct member or group of members with its individual effect. The elaboration and enrichments therefore became factors of the design, to be placed where they enhance it. These points are frequently forgotten or neglected, the parts being designed for themselves and not as being necessary elements of a well-conceived whole.

There are a few well-defined principles which should underlie all designs :

1. That the design have a dominating or central feature, or main idea or theme.

2. That the subordinate parts be treated as they are related to the main idea and so as to emphasize it.

3. That all parts of the work be kept clear, so that the working out of the theme be readily and easily comprehensible.

4. That enrichment be used as emphasis in its proper place and not for itself.

5. That the treatment and material harmonize, so that neither does violence to the other.

With these principles well mastered, facility and originality of idea will not militate against perfectly satisfactory results.

The plates in this work have been compiled so as to cover a large scope of interior design. They are given as suggestions as well as examples. From them may be gathered many ideas which may be used as motives for other compositions, as also for special articles of furnishing.

In execution they may be varied by the use of different or contrasting woods, and in many other ways that will readily suggest themselves.

ARCHITECTS AND DESIGNERS

Who have contributed to this work.

Mr. W. A. BATES,	NEW YORK.
Messrs. BURNHAM & ROOT,	CHICAGO.
Messrs. CABOT & CHANDLER,	BOSTON.
Mr. EDWARD DEWSON,	BOSTON.
Mr. C. A. GIFFORD,	NEW YORK.
Messrs. GOULD & ANGELL,	PROVIDENCE, R. I.
Mr. J. E. HUNTER,	NEW YORK.
Mr. GEO. MARTIN HUSS,	NEW YORK.
Mr. BRUCE PRICE,	NEW YORK.
Mr. W. S. PURDY,	NEW YORK.
Mr. J. PICKERING PUTNAM,	BOSTON.
Messrs. ROSSITER & WRIGHT,	NEW YORK.
Mr. WILLIAM B. TUTHILL,	NEW YORK.
Mr. F. F. WARD,	NEW YORK.
Mr. L. B. WHEELER,	NEW YORK.

Description of Plates.

FRONTISPIECE.—Mr. Bruce Price. Perspective view of the hall in the residence of Ashbel Greene, Englewood, N.J. At the extreme end the hall opens into the drawing-room; on the left is the sitting room, and the entrance to the garden. On the other side of garden entrance (not shown in the drawing) is the dining-room. The upper part of the walls of the garden entrance is filled with spindle-turned work, behind which, in each room, is a heavy hanging of tapestry, completely enclosing the rooms; in summer they may be thrown open for a free and delightful circulation of air. The hall is intended to be finished in black birch, which takes a beautiful finish; the wood is rich in tone and lovely in grain. The mantel is in Caen stone. The walls above the wainscot are to be rough sand finish, treated with a mottled conventional stamping, and then flat colored. A perspective sketch of the stairs is also given.

PLATE 2.—Mr. L. B. Wheeler. Entrance hall (perspective). This plate shows entrance hall opening into a staircase hall beyond. The fireplace is in stone; the frieze, shelf, panelling, &c., in mahogany or cherry. The stone used is Wyoming bluestone, pale buff sandstone, or a light limestone. The woodwork is finished in dead lustre. The panels at the head of chimney breast are filled with stained glass, and face on both halls. The soffit of the stairs is shown through the opening above fireplace partition. A library opens from staircase hall. A Caen stone fireplace, contrasted with woodwork in dark mahogany, and a hearth of vitreous sea-blue tiles would be very effective.

PLATE 3.—Details of Plate 2.

PLATE 4.—Messrs. Gould & Angell. Side of a hall, with details. (Elevation.) This design may be finished in cherry or any of the lighter hard woods. The face of the chimney breast above the mantel is to be set with glazed tiles in a single color (deep ultramarine green or olive). The seat may be covered with dark olive leather. The walls are to be painted a dark flat tone of olive. The doors may be glazed with plain or embossed glass.

PLATES 5 and 6.—Messrs. Burnham & Root. Plans and details of two staircase halls. They are designed to be erected in a light, hard wood, as oak or ash. The windows on the staircase (see plan) are to be filled with stained glass. Plate 5 also gives a design and detail for a ceiling in dark hard wood, cherry or mahogany.

PLATE 7.—Mr. Wm. A. Bates. Interior of hall showing fireplace, alcove and staircase. (Elevation.) The stairs are carried up over the alcove. The finish of the design is indicated on the plate.

PLATE 8.—Mr. L. B. Wheeler. Pen sketch of a staircase hall, with details. (Perspective).

PLATES 9 and 10.—Mr. J. E. Hunter. Hall suitable for a small country house in the Colonial style. (Elevation.) It may be effectively finished in any light hard wood. Plate 10 gives the details.

PLATE 11.—Messrs. Gould & Angell. Staircase and bay-window, and details. (Elevation.) This design is to be finished in oak with hard oil finish. The wall above the wainscot may be either papered or painted. The panels may be of Spanish white mahogany, which has a beautiful grain, and harmonizes well with the oak. They may be either polished or left the same as the oak.

PLATE 12.—Mr. C. A. Gifford. Staircase in a city house.

PLATE 13.—Details of Plate 12. This design would be well rendered in darkened oak.

PLATE 14.—Mr. Edward Dewson. Suggestions for staircases showing newels and part of runs. The upper designs may be executed either in dark or light woods. The lower design on the left will look best in light wood, as oak; that on the right in cherry or mahogany.

PLATE 15.—Messrs. Rossiter & Wright. Design for a staircase hall, with details. (Colonial style.) A light wood will be found suitable to this design.

PLATE 16.—Mr. Edward Dewson. Design for finish of parlor in cherry. Elevations of two sides of room and details are given.

PLATE 17.—Mr. L. B. Wheeler. Interior of library. (Perspective).

PLATE 18.—Mr. W. A. Bates. Interior of library (in Colonial style) showing mantel and bay window with plan and detail of frieze of mantel. (Elevation.) Oak, ash or butternut would be appropriate woods. The basket work above window is made by interlacing thin, flat strips of some pliable or elastic wood, as birch, ash, hazel, chestnut, which may be afterwards stained to match the other woodwork.

PLATE 19.—Messrs. Gould & Angell. Side of a library with details. (Elevation.) This design may be finished in cherry or mahogany. The book-shelves are to be covered in front with hangings, sliding on brass rods. The closet doors above shelves are to be filled with stained glass.

PLATE 20.—Mr. W. B. Tuthill. End of dining-room and details. (Elevation.) This design is to be executed in dark mahogany with slight lustre. The fireplace is to be framed with brass and small vitreous tiles of a dark turquoise color. The hearth, which fills the entire recess (see plan), is laid with glazed tiles in Venetian red. The walls are to be painted a dark olive grey with stencilled ornaments in a darker tone. Panels above mantel are of embossed leather. Above the shelves are two lateral windows in stained and jewelled glass; the centre is filled with bevelled mirror. The head of recess is filled with spindle screen. Two designs for flooring are shown in the plan.

PLATE 21.—Messrs. Gould & Angell. Side of dining-room and details. (Elevation.) Wood—cherry. Spandrils of arch are filled in with small wooden tiles, each of which has a turned or carved ornament. The sideboard is also in cherry; upper panel is of stamped leather, that under it a bevelled mirror.

PLATE 22.—Mr. Edward Dewson. A café interior. (Perspective.) This plate also gives an elevation of the mantel and a plan of the room.

PLATE 23.—Details, furniture and fittings of café. (Plate 22.) Notes of finish are given on this plate.

PLATE 24.—Mr. George Martin Huss. Office of estate of Wm. C. Rhinelander, Esq., deceased. The plate includes plan, staircase, partitions, mantel, &c. The style of finish is noted on the plate.

PLATE 25.—Mr. J. Pickering Putnam. Chimney piece in a city house, with details. The face of chimney breast, as indicated, is to be filled with small glazed tiles of color to harmonize or contrast with surrounding woodwork. The panels on either side are openings to ventilators, and are of perforated metal.

PLATE 26.—Mr. Edward Dewson. Design for two wood mantels, with details.

PLATE 27.—Mr. Edward Dewson. Sketches of four small mantels, with details. These designs may be well executed in a variety of woods, and be varied by the omission or interchange of parts.

PLATE 28.—Messrs. Rossiter & Wright. Designs for mantels of low cost, with details. These may be finished in hard woods, or in pine oiled or painted.

PLATE 29.—Messrs. Cabot & Chandler. Designs for two mantels; also designs for wainscoting.

PLATE 30.—Mr. Edward Dewson. Interior and exterior doors; seven designs.

PLATE 31.—Messrs. Gould & Angell. Examples of window and door finish.

PLATE 32.—Messrs. Rossiter & Wright. Designs for doors, with details.

PLATE 33.—Mr. W. S. Purdy. Designs for trims of doors and other openings, with details and sections.

PLATE 34.—Messrs. Rossiter & Wright. Wood and plaster cornices (one-half full size).

PLATE 35.—Messrs. Gould & Angell. Wood ceiling; four designs with details.

PLATE 36.—Messrs. Rossiter & Wright. Designs for wainscots, with details.

PLATE 37.—Messrs. Gould & Angell. Examples of panelling for wainscots, ceilings, &c.

PLATE 38.—Messrs. Rossiter & Wright. Hall furniture and details, including designs for hat-rack, hall table, chair, &c.

PLATE 39.—Messrs. Rossiter & Wright. Designs for bookcases. The first design has an open, the second a closed front. The third design is intended to be built in between the chimney breast and wall, a similar one (reversed) being placed on the other side of breast.

PLATE 40.—Messrs. Rossiter & Wright. Dining-room furniture, containing design for two sideboards, one of which is planned to be placed in a corner.

PLATE 41.—Mr. W. S. Purdy. Dining-room furniture, including sideboard (built in), with details. A plan of a ceiling in wood and plaster is also given.

PLATE 42.—Mr. Edward Dewson. Suggestions for bank or counting-room finish in hard wood, with details.

PLATE 43.—Mr. Wm. B. Tuthill. Details for drug store, including wall-cases, cashier's and prescription desks, and two designs for letter boxes. Wood—cherry. The open work at head of wall-cases forms the doors of closets. The lattice of cashier's desk is of turned cherry spindles and strips of birch stained to match.

PLATE 44.—Mr. Wm. B. Tuthill. Details for drug store, giving four designs for counters, and a design for show case. The upper part of case is open, and the central part closed on all sides with glass doors. The space below is partly filled in with a spindle lattice, making a receptacle for sponges.

PLATE 45.—Messrs. Rossiter & Wright. Screens for stores, offices, &c.

PLATE 46.—Messrs. Gould & Angell. Drug store fixtures, showing wall-cases, counters, &c. A dark wood would suit this design.

PLATE 47.—Messrs. Rossiter & Wright. Fittings for a drug store, comprising open shelf-cases, cashier's desk, table-counters, chairs, &c., with details.

PLATE 48.—Mr. W. S. Purdy. Store fittings, including designs for shelving, panelled and table-counters, cashier's desk, with details.

PLATE 49.—Messrs. Gould & Angell. Bar-room and details (Elevation.)

PLATE 50.—Mr. F. F. Ward. Finish of an apartment house. The plate includes a plan of the apartment, and designs and details for main stairs and doors.

PLATE 51.—Mr. F. F. Ward. Finish of an apartment house, giving designs and details for parlor and dining-room mantels.

PLATE 52.—Mr. F. F. Ward. Finish of an apartment house, giving hall wainscot, designs and details of doors, kitchen dresser, &c.

NOTES ON WOOD FINISH.

A great part of the effect of any piece of decorative wood-work depends upon the description and method of its ultimate finish.

Variety and differences of tone, contrasts between the natural color and that which can be legitimately given, enrichment of plainer and emphasis to the more naturally beautiful woods, effects which can be almost endlessly varied, may be obtained by simple mechanical treatment.

From the following memoranda, collected from various sources, many suggestions may be taken.

The woods in general use for the construction and finish (including furniture) of houses may be classed as follows:

For General Construction,—Pine, oak, whitewood, chestnut, ash, spruce, sycamore.

For Ordinary Finish.—Beech, birch, cedar, cherry, pine, white-wood.

For Best Finish.—Cherry, mahogany, maple, oak, rosewood, satin-wood, sandal wood, chestnut, cedar, tulip wood, walnut, ebony, butternut, white mahogany.

The better known woods are classified according to the properties for which they are most valued, as follows:

Elasticity.—Ash, hazel, hickory, lancewood, chestnut, snakewood, yew.

Elasticity and Toughness.—Beech, elm, lignumvitæ, oak, walnut, hornbeam.

Even Grain (for carving and engraving).—Pear, pine, box, lime tree.

Durability. (In dry work).—Cedar, oak, poplar, yellow pine. (Exposed to weather)—chestnut, larch, and locust.

Coloring Matters. *Red*—Brazil wood, camwood, logwood, red sanders, sapan wood. *Yellow.*—Fustic, Zante.

Scent.—Camphor wood, cedar, rosewood, sandal wood, satinwood, sassafras.

There are several imported woods which are used only decoratively, such as amaranth, amboyna, zebra wood.

The woods best adapted for ebonizing are given variously by different authorities; among them may be mentioned, pear, holly, beech, chestnut, cherry, sycamore, plane.

The woods most commonly used for inlaying are, ebony, box, palm, bird's eye maple, beech, satinwood, sandalwood, holly.

Veneers are cut from most hard woods, especially the more costly. The burs or gnarls of hardwood trees give beautiful veneers on account of the irregularity of the grain. The junction of large roots and large branches with the trunk of the tree also gives good veneers. Of this class is the French walnut, Hungarian ash, &c.

VARNISHES.

Varnishing to be thoroughly successful should not be done in a cold room, the proper temperature being 70° or 80° F.

It is seldom, if ever, necessary to specify the composition of the varnishes used in ordinary work, most of them being used prepared by the manufacturer. A few formulæ, however, may prove serviceable.

Body copal varnish for parts requiring to be polished: 8 parts copal, 3½ oil of turpentine, 2 linseed oil.

Cabinet varnish: 7 parts copal, 3 oil of turpentine, ½ linseed oil.

White varnish for furniture: white wax, dissolved by heat in oil of turpentine, 1 pint; or 6 parts of white wax dissolved in 48 parts of petroleum. It should be applied while warm, and allowed to cool. It may then be polished with a coarse flannel cloth.

Mahogany varnish. This varnish brings out the grain strongly, and imparts a rich red tone to the wood.

Gum sandarach, 2 oz.; shellac, 1 oz.; gum benjamin, ½ oz.; Venice turpentine, 1 oz.; spirits of wine, 1 pint.

This may be toned red with Dragon's blood, or yellow with saffron.

The gum should be slowly dissolved and strained.

Varnished work may be finished with a lustre (not a glassy surface) by applying three or more coats of hard varnish, each coat being allowed to dry thoroughly, and then rubbing the work down carefully with pulverized pumice stone and water, applied with a soft rag.

Ordinary varnishes may be toned to match the wood by the addition of various coloring matters. This will frequently improve the appearance of the finish.

There are several patented preparations, called "wood-fillers," which are used in preparing the surface of woodwork previous to the final oiling or varnishing. They are known under the names of their patentees, as Hojer, Wheeler, &c. Their purpose is to fill up the pores of the wood level with the solid parts, forming a hard, smooth, durable surface, leaving the wood its natural color, clean and brilliant. The particles which fill and harden in the pores are not visible.

Ordinary oil or varnish finish may follow its application. The "fillers" are manufactured in different colors, so that they may be used on any of the hard woods, namely, for oak or other light woods, light and dark walnut, light and dark mahogany, rosewood and ebony. There is also a "transparent" filler, which may be used on any wood, irrespective of color.

The "filler" is to be thinned with turpentine to the consistency of varnish, and applied with a brush or sponge, and when it becomes flat, rub it across the grain with Excelsior shavings or grass fibre. The corners and hollows in mouldings and carving should then be cleaned out with a stiff bristle brush or stick.

The work must be thoroughly wiped off with a cotton cloth.

No oil should be used with the filler. It will require at least twelve hours for the filler to dry perfectly hard.

Raw oil only should be used with natural woods. It is more volatile than boiled oil, and penetrates readily into the grain, forming a hard resinous filling.

Mixed with a small quantity of turpentine, and well rubbed in, it improves most woods. A little color ground in the oil will also be of advantage.

POLISHING.

Soft woods may be turned so smooth as to require no other polish than that which can be given by holding fine shavings of the same wood against them in the lathe.

For polishing mahogany, walnut and some other woods, the following formula is given: dissolve beeswax by heat in spirits of turpentine, until the mixture becomes viscid. Apply by a clean cloth, and rub thoroughly with another flannel or cloth.

Beeswax is sometimes alone used. For work in position, it must be melted and applied and rubbed as above. For work in the lathe, it can be applied by friction, the slight amount of wax melted being sufficient for the polish. The work should be thoroughly rubbed.

Mahogany may be polished by rubbing first with linseed oil, and then by cloth dipped in very fine brick dust. (Nearly all mahogany furniture in England is polished in this way.)

Some hard woods have a natural polish, and do not require a polishing medium.

A fine gloss can be produced by rubbing with linseed oil, and then holding turnings or shavings of the same material against the work in the lathe.

A very perfect surface can be obtained with glass-paper, which, if followed by hard rubbing, will give a beautiful lustre.

Lustre can also be given to carefully finished surfaces, by applying a small quantity of thinned varnish, shellac or "fillers," by a cloth, and carefully and thoroughly rubbing.

By contrasting the several methods of natural finish, very beautiful effects can be obtained.

The natural color of woods may be darkened and improved, and the figure of the grain emphasized, by several means.

The darkeners in general use are, logwood, lime, brown soft-soap, dyed oil, aqua fortis, sulphate of iron, nitrate of silver exposed to the sun's rays, carbonate of soda, bichromate and permanganate of potash, and other preparations of an acidulous or alkaline nature. The last three are preferable, and are prepared as follows: One ounce of one of the alkalies is powdered and dissolved in two gills of boiling water. Dilute with water to the required tone. Apply with sponge or flannel, saturating the surface, and immediately dry with soft rags.

The solution of the carbonate is used for the dark woods, as rosewood; that of the bichromate, for all intermediate and white woods, as mahogany, oak, beech.

The grain of hard woods, especially mahogany and rosewood, is well brought out by rubbing with spirits of hartshorn, and then with oil, which may or may not be colored.

A red oil, which is specially adapted to discolored mahogany or rosewood, may be prepared as follows: Soak alkanet root in linseed oil for ten or twelve hours, and then press the oil through a cloth bag. This may be used as a coloring matter for other oil, and will give a beautiful red tone.

The lightest hard woods, *e. g.*, birch, may be improved in color by oil tinged with rose madder or Venetian red.

Maple and some few other woods can be bleached by a strong solution of oxalic acid in hot water, to which a few drops of nitre has been added.

The grain of yellow pine can be well brought out by two or three coats of japan, much diluted with turpentine, and afterwards oiled and rubbed.

The effect of age may be given to mahogany or walnut by lime-water, applied before oiling or varnishing.

STAINING.

The best, clearest, and most satisfactory work is obtained by repeated light coats of the stain, in the same manner as " washes " with water colors.

Before the first coat is applied, the work should be carefully prepared with glass paper, all small holes and cracks being filled, and the surface brushed free from all dust. Before each subsequent application of the stain, the surface of the work should be carefully cleaned.

In staining soft woods it will be found advantageous to use a priming coat, either of an ordinary varnish or japan, strongly diluted with turpentine.

A coat of wood fillers would perhaps be better.

The pores of the wood are thus filled and a good solid surface is given on which to work. Much less subsequent labor will be needed for producing the required result.

Preparations are sometimes used to improve and enhance the stains. Some of them are as follows: Mix one ounce of nitric acid, one-half teaspoonful hydrochloric acid, one-quarter ounce of grain tin, and two ounces of distilled water. It is to stand two days before being used.

For satinwood stain, spirits of nitre; for oak stain, a strong solution of oxalic acid; for mahogany stain, dilute nitrous acid.

MAHOGANY STAINS.

1. Two ounces of dragon's blood dissolved in one quart of rectified spirits of wine. Shake frequently while dissolving.

2. Give the woodwork a priming coat of japan, thinned with turpentine, then two or more coats of burnt sienna, toned with French ochre, in turpentine, with a small quantity of oil.

3. Raw sienna in beer. Add burnt sienna to obtain required tone.

4. For light mahogany stain, dissolve two ounces of dragon's blood in one quart of oil of turpentine; warm and shake.

For Dark Mahogany Stain.

5. Boil one-half pound of madder and two ounces of logwood chips in one gallon of water. Brush the decoction, while hot, well over the work. When dry, paint with a solution of two drams of pearlash in one quart of water.

6. Boil one pound of Brazil wood in one gallon of water for three hours; add one ounce of pearlash, and apply while hot.

Brush over with a solution of two ounces of alum in one quart of water.

Maple is readily stained to imitate mahogany.

RED STAINS.

A good red stain, for common work, such as chairs, can obtained by using archil. If, however, after one or two coa it is brushed over with a hot solution of pearlash in water, t color will be improved.

Camwood dust in rectified naphtha gives a good red stain

Violin Crimson.

Boil one pound of Brazil-wood dust in three quarts of wa for one hour. Strain and add one-half ounce of cochineal. B again gently for a short time.

If a more scarlet tint is required, boil one-half an ounc saffron in a quart of water for one hour, and pass it over previous stain.

(For red stains, see also mahogany stains.)

Rosewood Stain.

In three pints of water boil one-half pound of logwood decoction is of a dark red color; then add one-half ounc salts of tartar.

Three or four coats are required, each of which mus boiling hot, and be allowed to dry thoroughly before anoth applied.

BROWN STAINS.

A hot decoction of logwood or Brazil wood, or both combined, give brown stains. The second gives a mahogany brown, the first a dark brown.

A solution of permanganate of potash forms a rapid and excellent stain. When spread on pear or cherry wood for a few minutes, it forms a permanent dark brown, which, after careful washing, drying, oiling and polishing, shows a beautiful reddish tone. The dull color becomes very rich by oiling and rubbing. This stain is known as the "Swedish stain."

A brown stain can be obtained by boiling one part of catechu, cutch or gambier with thirty parts of water and a little soda. It should be allowed to thoroughly dry in the air, and be painted over with a solution of one part of bichromate of potash in thirty parts of water.

By varying the strength of the solution, various shades may be given to these materials, which will be permanent and tend to preserve the wood.

WALNUT STAIN.

Boil one and one-half ounces of washing soda, one-quarter of an ounce of bichromate of potash, in one quart of water, and add two and one-half ounces of Vandyke brown.

This solution may be used either hot or cold.

Boxwood and some of the lighter very hard woods may be stained brown by heating gently and treating with aqua fortis. The heat must be maintained until staining is completed. The work must then be oiled and polished.

OAK STAIN.

Dissolve two ounces of American potash and two ounces of pearlash in one quart of water. Dilute with water to required tone.

A solution of asphaltum in spirits of turpentine gives a good brown stain for coarse oaken work.

Yellow stains can be produced by the application of a solution of gamboge or tumeric in alcohol, or barberry root boiled in water. These may be diluted or strengthened as required.

Dilute nitric acid will also give a yellow stain to wood.

EBONIZING AND BLACK STAINS.

All work that is to be ebonized must be thoroughly smoothed and cleansed from all dust and irregularities.

Pass over the surface to be ebonized two or more coats of a hot decoction of logwood or Brazil wood, each coat being allowed to become thoroughly dry. Then paint over with one or more coats of a solution of sulphate of iron. Rub and polish.

Or, boil one-half pound of logwood chips and one ounce of pearlash in three quarts of water. Apply hot.

Then boil one-half pound of logwood in three quarts of water, and add one-half ounce each of verdigris and copperas. Strain, and add one-half pound of rusty steel filings and powdered nutgalls.

This stain is available for immediate use.

Or, to six quarts of water add one pound of logwood and two or three handfuls of fresh walnut peelings. Boil till reduced to one-half the quantity and strain; add one pint of the best vinegar, boil again, and apply hot.

Dissolve one ounce of copperas in one quart of water, and apply this hot over the previous stain.

Each coat must be allowed to dry thoroughly.

Strong nitric acid will also give a black stain.

Note.—Among the works consulted for the above notes are Encyclop. Brit., 9th Ed.; Am. Encyclop.; Spon's "Workshop Receipts;" Stokes' "Cabinet-maker;" the "Manufacturer and Builder," &c., &c.

Late Victorian Interiors

and Interior Details

Interior of Hall designed by . . . . . L. B. Wheeler . Architect . 145 B'way . N.

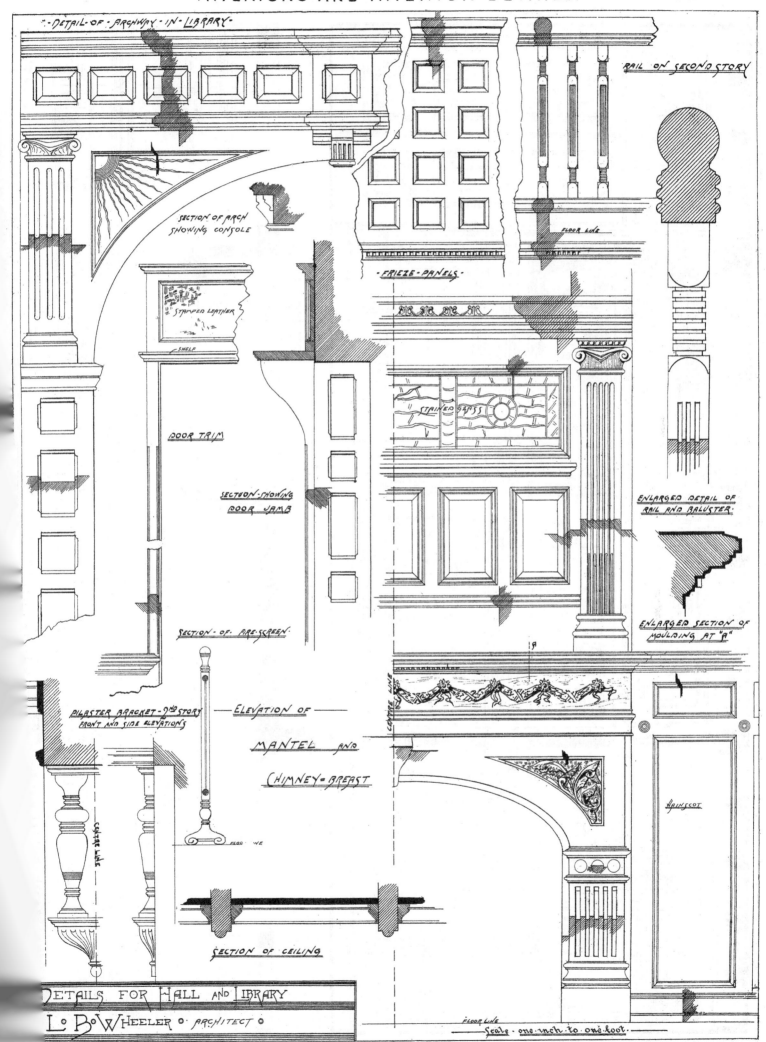

DETAIL OF ARCHWAY IN LIBRARY

RAIL ON SECOND STORY

SECTION OF ARCH SHOWING CONSOLE

FLOOR LINE

FRIEZE PANELS

STAMPED LEATHER

SHELF

DOOR TRIM

STAINED GLASS

SECTION SHOWING DOOR JAMB

ENLARGED DETAIL OF RAIL AND BALUSTER

SECTION OF FIRE SCREEN

ENLARGED SECTION OF MOULDING AT "A"

PILASTER BRACKET 2ND STORY FRONT AND SIDE ELEVATIONS

ELEVATION OF

MANTEL AND

CHIMNEY BREAST

WAINSCOT

CENTRE LINE

FLOOR LINE

SECTION OF CEILING

DETAILS FOR HALL AND LIBRARY

L. B. WHEELER ○ ARCHITECT ○

FLOOR LINE

Scale one inch to one foot

DETAIL OF OVER-MANTEL

PLAN OF FIRE PLACE AND HEARTH

DETAIL OF MANTEL

CHELSEA TILES

SIDE OF A HALL.
SCALE OF ELEVATIONS ½ IN.= 1 FT.
SCALE OF DETAILS 1 IN. = 1 FT.

SEAT

TABLE

ARM OF SEAT

PLAN OF A
HALL CEILING

— SCALE · 4 FEET TO 1 INCH —

ALTERNATIVE SECTION

SECTION OF CEILING BEAM
AND ELEVATION OF BRACKET "A"

SECTION

DETAILS OF
STAIRCASE HALL

HALF PLAN OF CEILING PANEL

CENTRE LINE

PLAN

SCALE — 1½ FEET TO 1 INCH

WAINSCOT · IN
HALL

6' 6"

DOOR TRIM

INTERIOR DETAILS

— BURNHAM & ROOT — ARCHITECTS —

— SCALE · 1 INCH TO 1 FOOT —

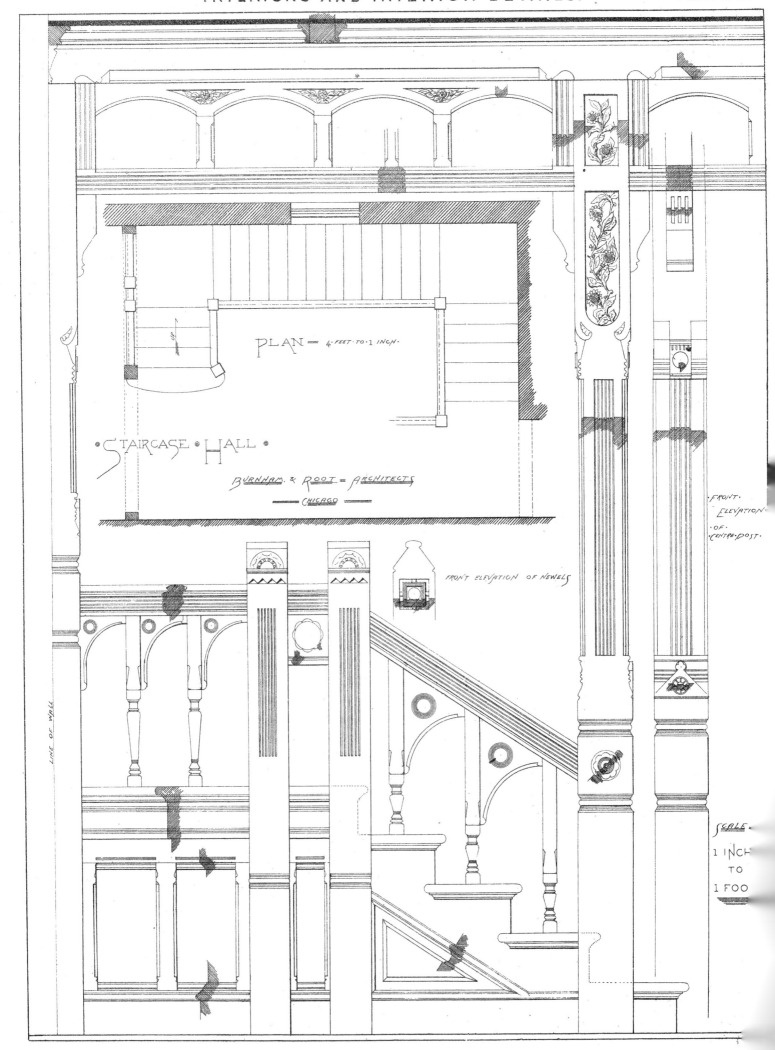

PLAN = 4 FEET TO 1 INCH.

·STAIRCASE · HALL ·

BURNHAM & ROOT = ARCHITECTS

CHICAGO

·FRONT·
·ELEVATION·
·OF·
·CENTRE·POST·

FRONT ELEVATION OF NEWELS

SCALE·
1 INCH
TO
1 FOOT

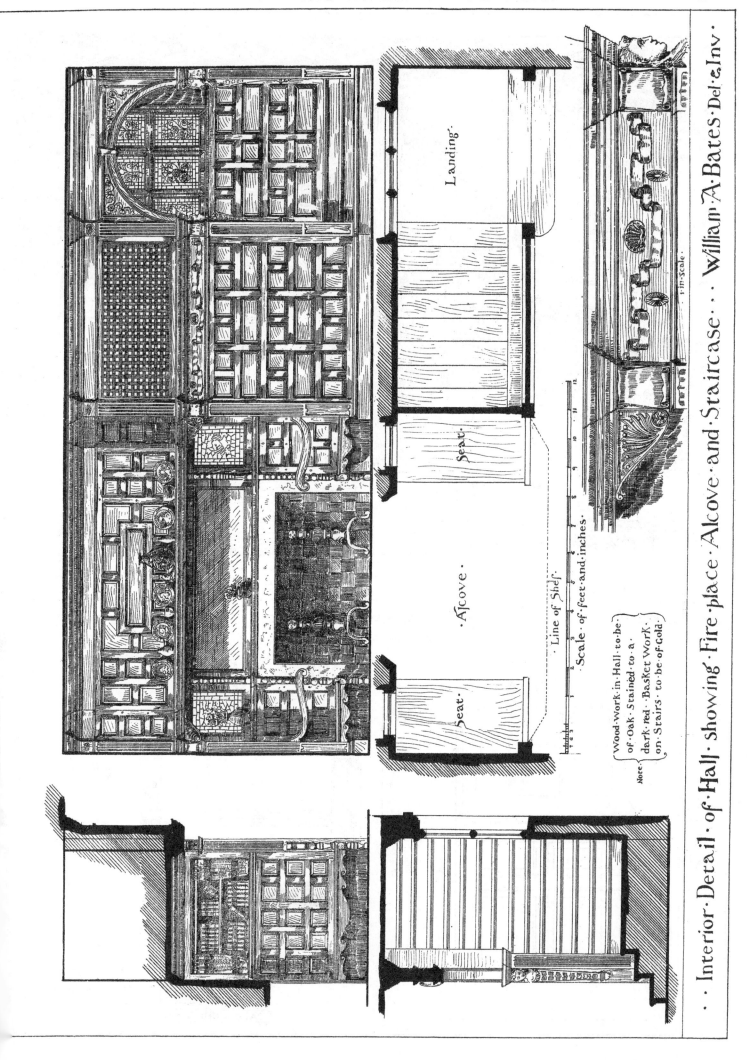

Landing.

Seat.

Alcove.

Seat.

Alcove.

Seat.

Line of Shelf.

Scale of feet and inches.

1 in Scale.

Note.

Wood work in Hall to be of Oak Stained to a dark red. Basket Work on Stairs to be of Gold.

Interior Detail of Hall showing Fire place Alcove and Staircase . . . William A. Bates Del & Inv.

STAIRCASE·HALL · ·   · L·B·WHEELER · · · ARCH'T

DETAIL OF HEAD OF POST

SHELF

BRACKET

DETAIL OF PANELING AT STAIR LANDING

CORNER POST

DETAIL OF CROSS·BEAM

DETAIL OF FRIEZE

THIS SPACE·TO·BE DECORATED EITHER IN COLOR OR EMBOSSED WORK

SECTION AT "R"

[SCALE · 3 IN = 1 FT]

DETAIL OF NEWEL AND BALUSTER

ROUND

SQUARE

SCALE = ONE = INCH = TO = ONE = FOOT =

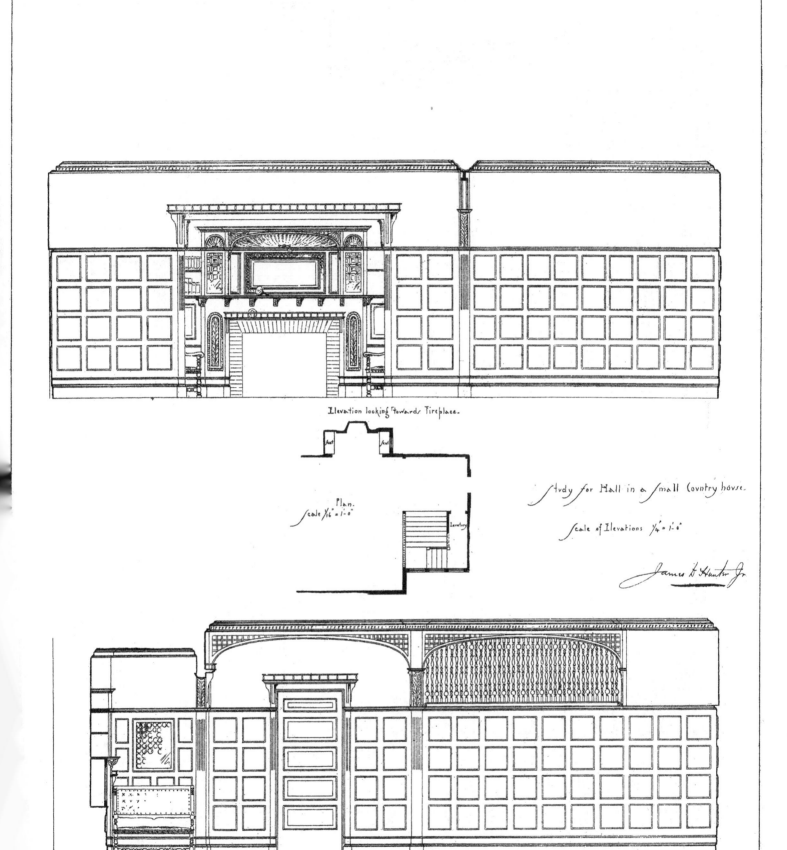

Elevation looking towards Fireplace.

Plan.
Scale 1/16" = 1'-0"

Study for Hall in a small Country house.

Scale of Elevations 1/4" = 1'-0"

James D. Hunter Jr.

Elevation looking towards Staircase.

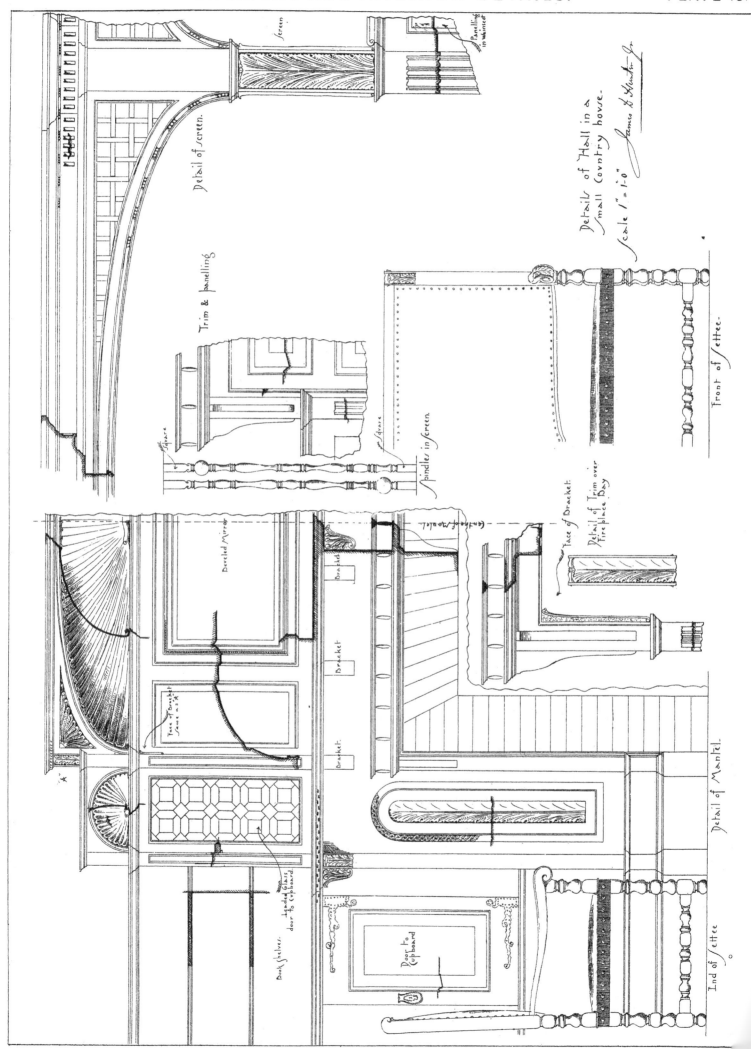

Detail of Hall in a small Country house.

Scale 1" = 1'-0"

James G. Hunter Jr.

Detail of screen.

Screen.

Panelling in Wainscot

Trim & panelling

Spindles in screen.

Square

Square

Front of settee.

Beveled Mirror

Bracket

Bracket

Bracket

Face of Bracket same as A

Bookshelves.

Leaded Glass door to Cupboard

Door to Cupboard

Detail of Mantel.

End of settee

Face of Bracket.

Detail of Trim over Fireplace Bay

(End face of Mantel.)

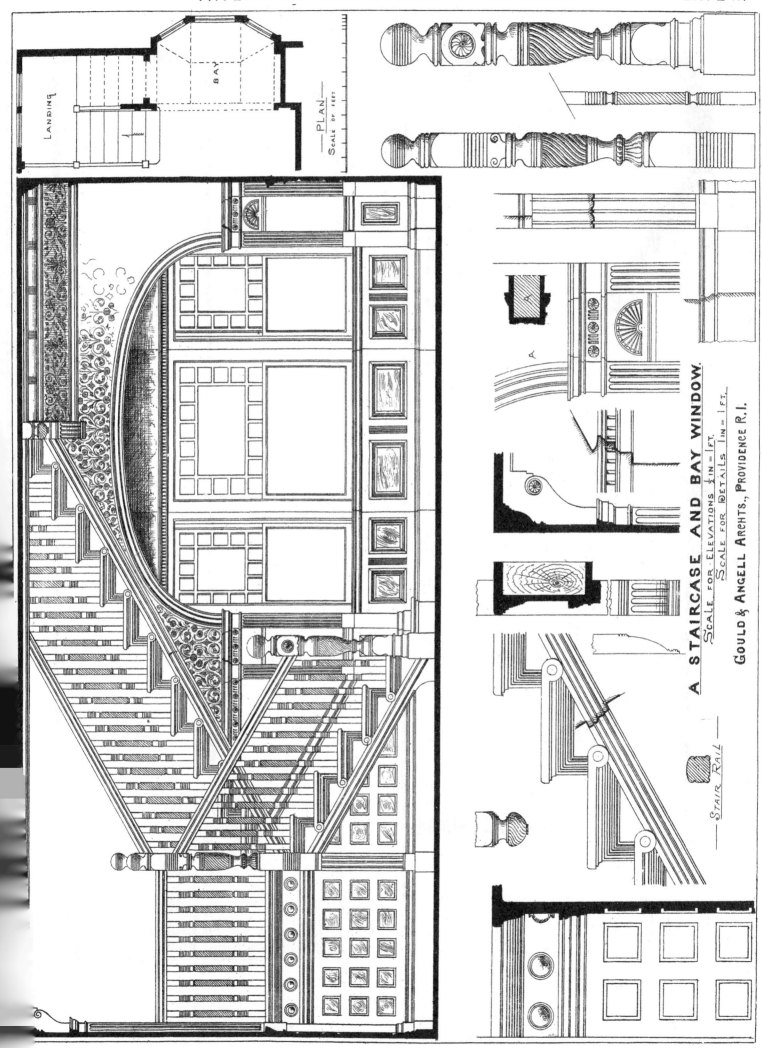

LANDING

BAY

PLAN
Scale of Feet

A STAIRCASE AND BAY WINDOW.

Scale for Elevations ½in.=1ft.

Scale for Details 1in.=1ft.

GOULD & ANGELL ARCHTS., PROVIDENCE R.I.

STAIR RAIL

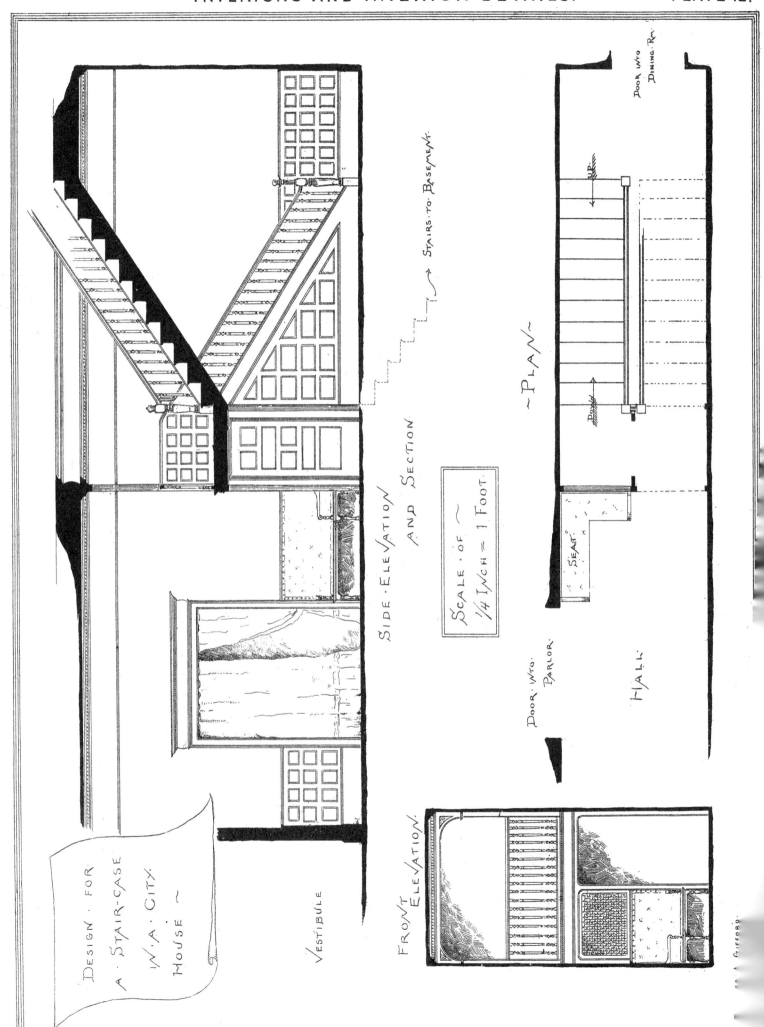

Design for a Stair-case W. A. City House ~

Vestibule

Side Elevation and Section

Stairs to Basement.

Scale of ¼ Inch = 1 Foot

~ Plan ~

Door into Dining Rm.

Up

Down

Seat

Door into Parlor.

Hall.

Front Elevation.

W. A. Gifford.

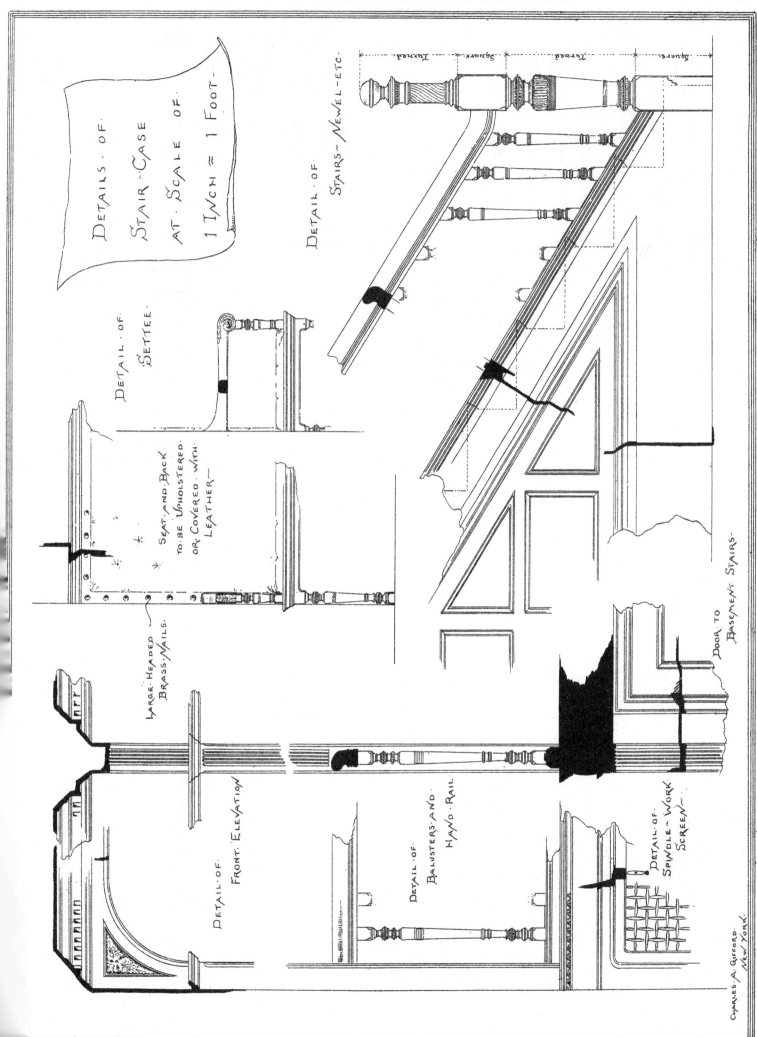

DETAILS · OF · STAIR · CASE · AT · SCALE · OF · 1 INCH = 1 FOOT ·

DETAIL · OF · STAIRS~ NEWEL~ ETC ·

DETAIL · OF · SETTEE ·

SEAT · AND · BACK · TO · BE · UPHOLSTERED · OR · COVERED · WITH · LEATHER~

LARGE · HEADED · BRASS · NAILS ·

DETAIL · OF · FRONT · ELEVATION ·

DETAIL · OF · BALUSTERS · AND · HAND · RAIL ·

DOOR · TO · BASEMENT · STAIRS ·

DETAIL · OF · SPINDLE~ WORK · SCREEN~

Turned   Square   Turned   Square

CHARLES · A · GIFFORD · NEW · YORK ·

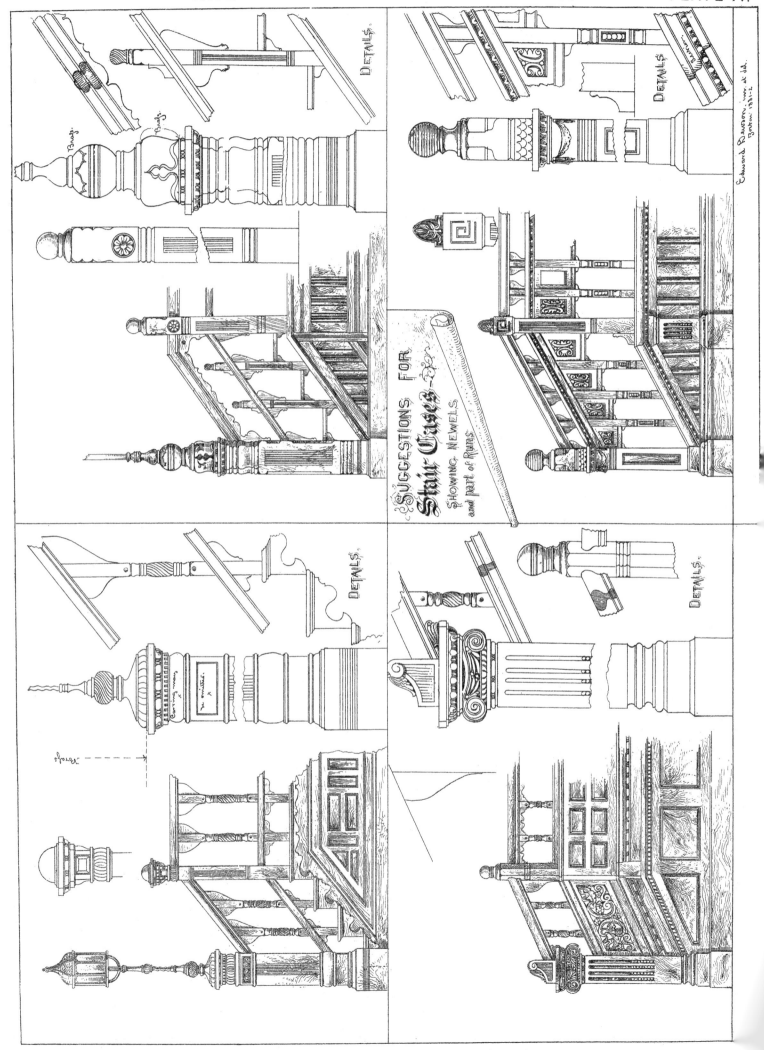

SUGGESTIONS FOR Stair Cases SHOWING NEWELS and part of Runs

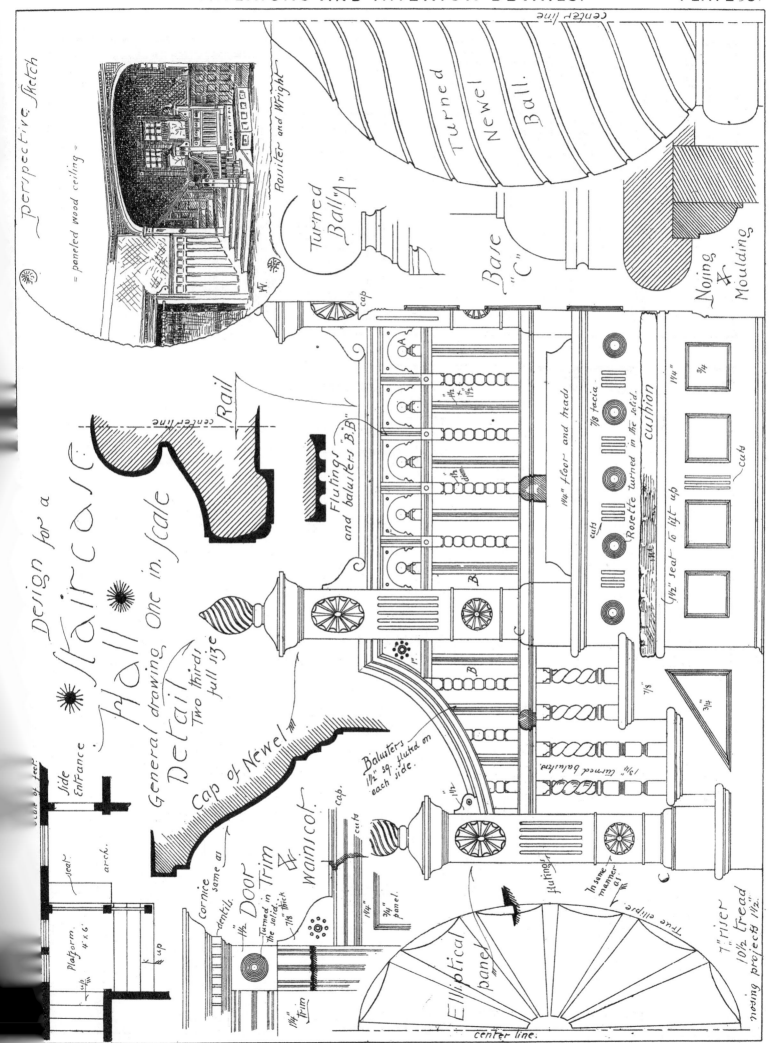

Design for a
Staircase *Hall* *

General drawing, one in. scale
Detail Two thirds full size

perspective sketch

= paneled wood ceiling =

Rossiter and Wright

Turned Newel Ball.

Turned "Ball A"

Base "C"

Nosing & Moulding

Rail

centre line

Flutings and balusters "B.B"

A

cap

1¼ x 1½

1¼ diam.

B

B

C

⅞ facia

Rosette turned in the solid.

cushion

1¼ floor and treads

cuts

4½" seat to lift up

1¼"

¾

cuts

⅛

1¾" turned balusters

Cap of Newel

cap.

Balusters
1½" sq. fluted on each side.

1½

Door Trim & Wainscot.

cornice same as dentil.

Turned in the solid. 1⅞" thick

1¼"

¾ panel.

1¼" Trim

cuts

1½

flutings

In some manner as

True ellipse

Elliptical panel

7"riser 10½" tread
nosing projects 1½.

center line.

Side Entrance

arch.

seat.

Platform 4 x 6

up

up

scale of feet

Door in alcove. Wood Mantel. Window. Side of Cabinet.

Window in side of alcove. Side of mantel. Bay Window. Parlor Cabinet.

Scale for Elevations.

Scale for Details.

.:PARLOR FINISHED IN CHERRY SHOWING TWO SIDES OF THE ROOM:.
.WITH DETAILS.

LIBRARY · DESIGNED BY · L. B. WHEELER · ARCHITECT

· DETAILS OF CHIMNEY-PIECE ·

· SCALE ·

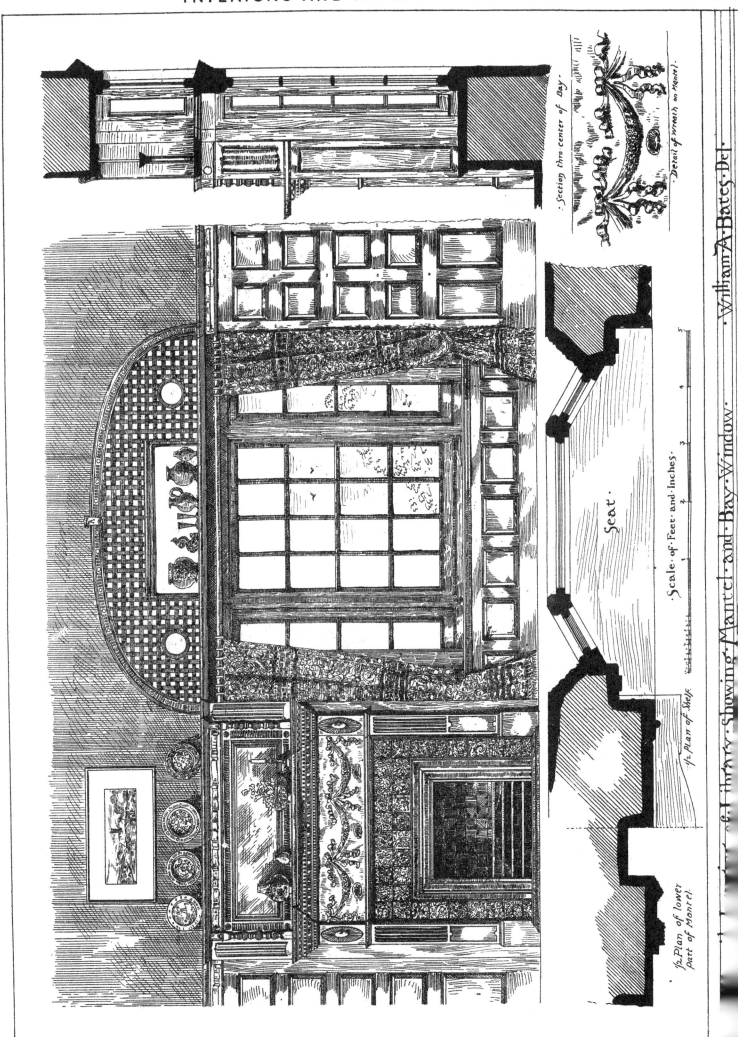

Section thro center of Bay.

Detail of wreath on Mantel.

Seat.

Scale of Feet and Inches.

Plan of Shelf.

Plan of lower part of Mantel.

Library Showing Mantel and Bay Window.

William A. Bates. Del.

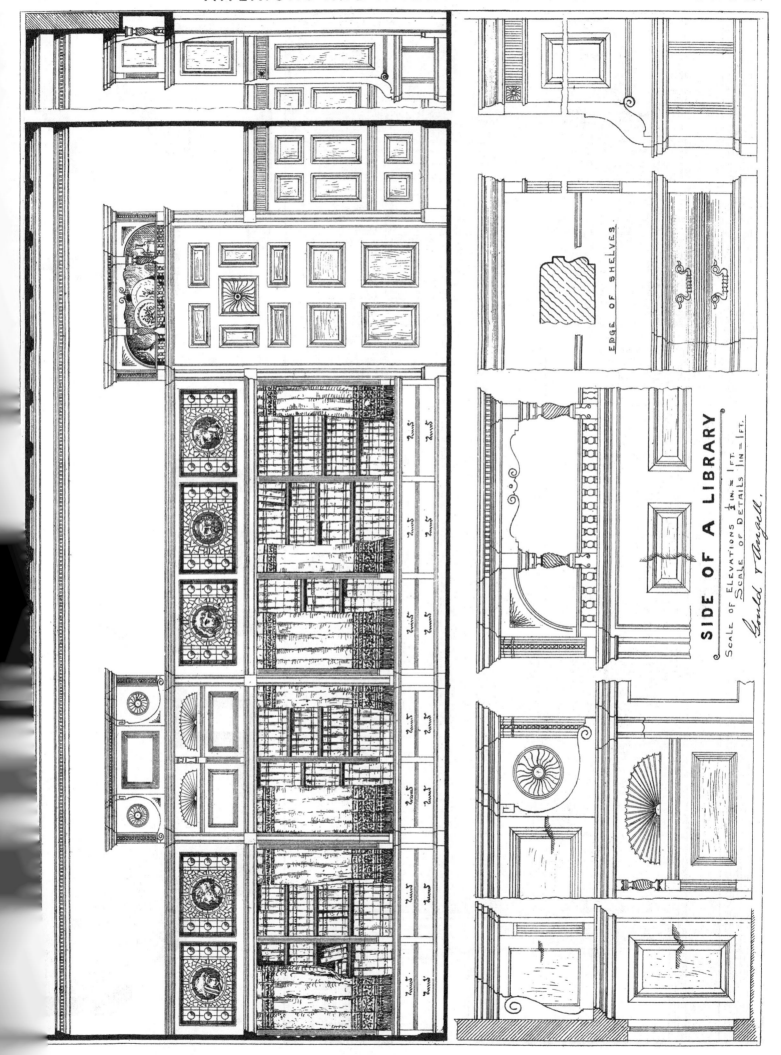

EDGE OF SHELVES.

SIDE OF A LIBRARY

Scale of Elevations ½ in. = 1 ft.
Scale of Details 1 in. = 1 ft.

Gould & Angell.

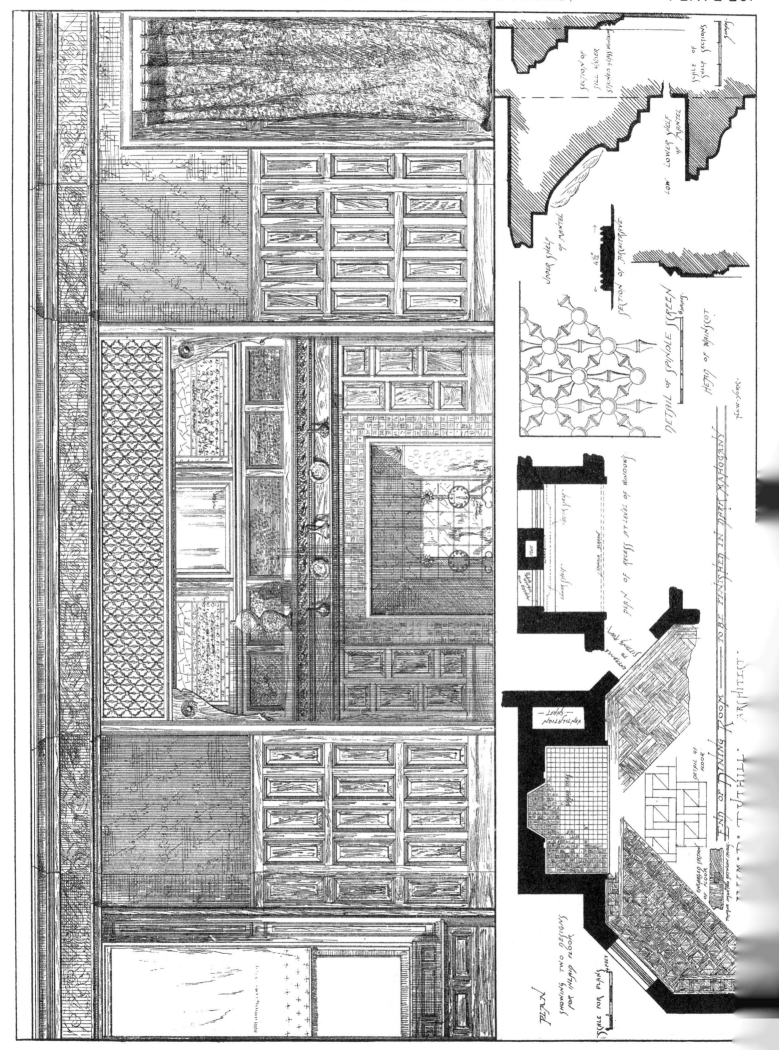

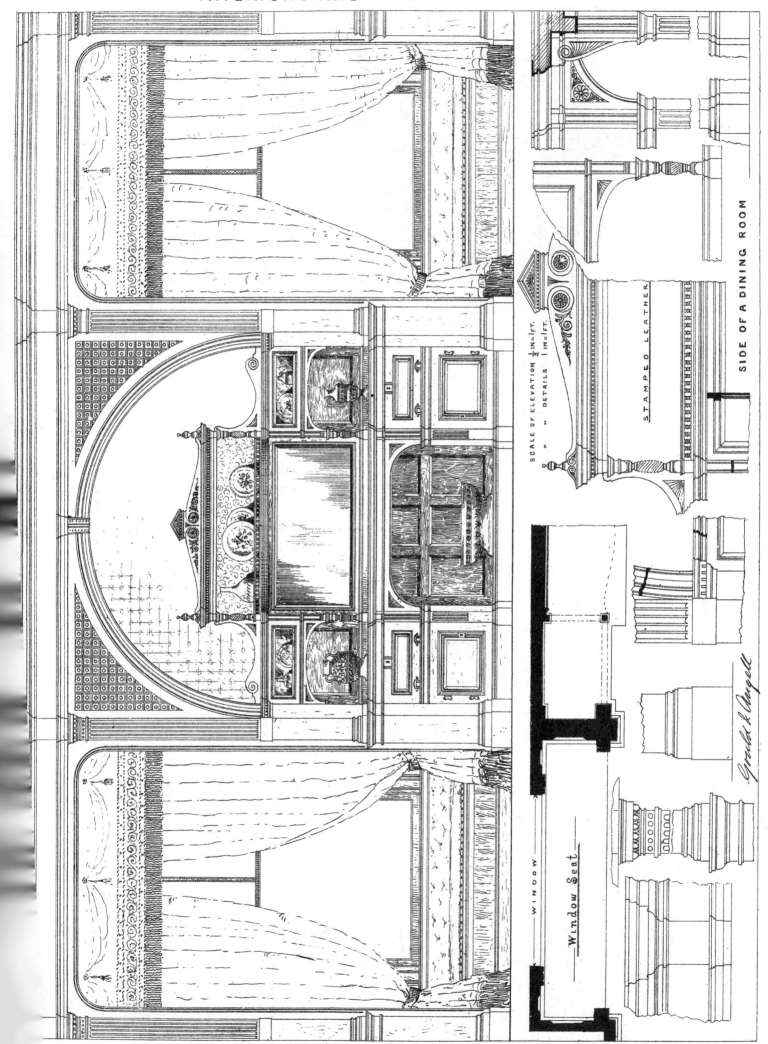

SCALE OF ELEVATION ½ IN.=1 FT.
" " DETAILS 1 IN.=1 FT.

STAMPED LEATHER

SIDE OF A DINING ROOM

WINDOW

Window Seat

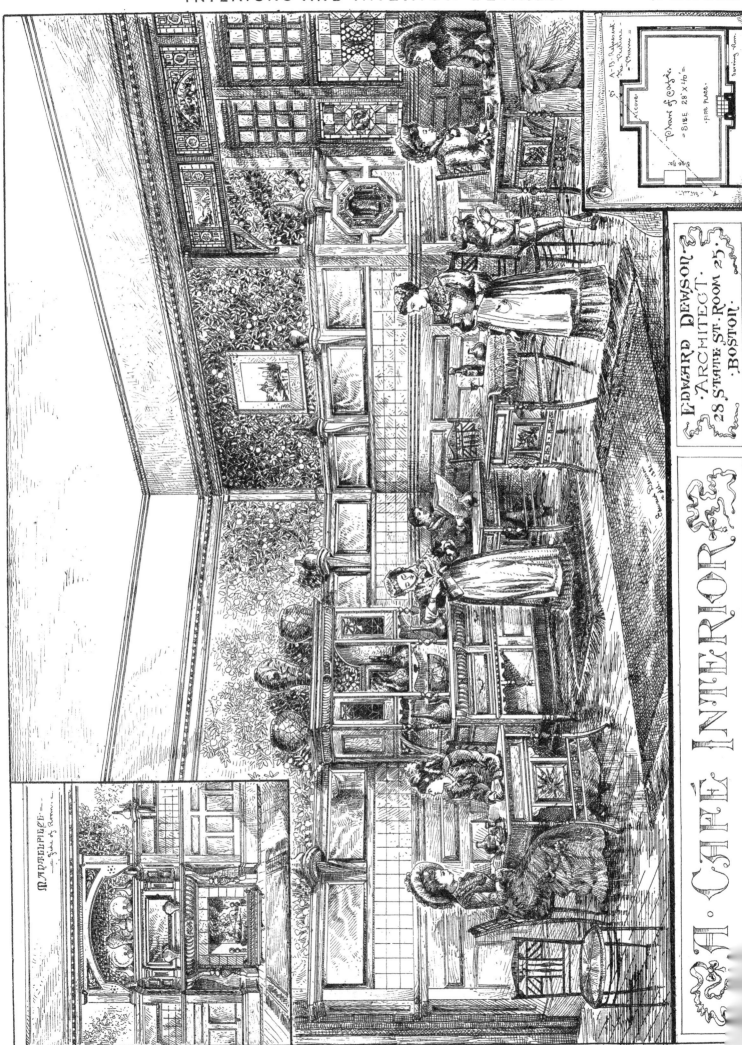

A CAFÉ INTERIOR.

Edward Dewson.
ARCHITECT.
28 STATE ST. ROOM 25.
BOSTON.

MANTELPIECE.

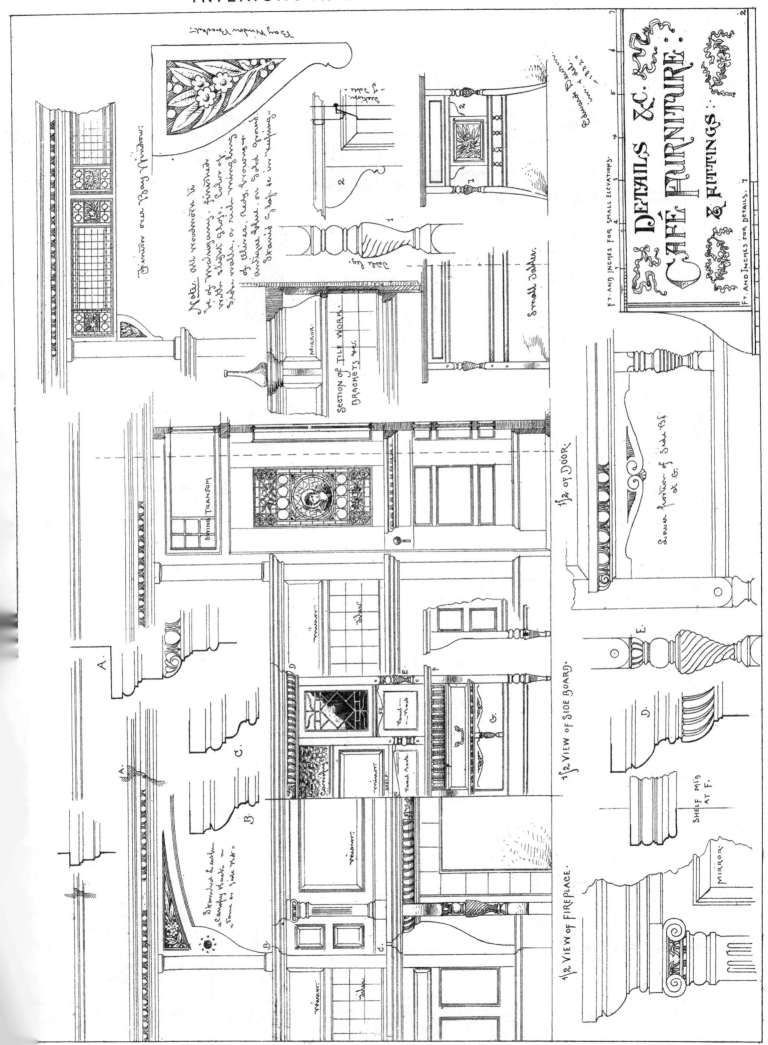

DETAILS &c.
CAFÉ FURNITURE
& FITTINGS.

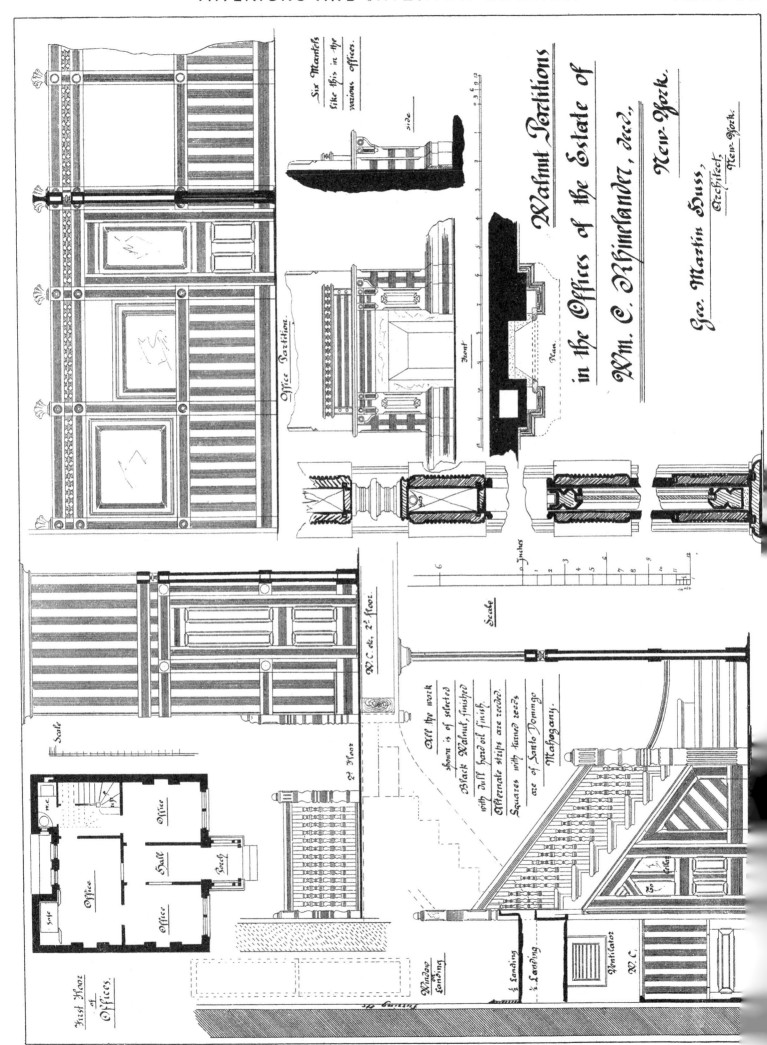

Walnut Partitions

in the Offices of the Estate of

Wm. C. Rhinelander, dec'd.,

New-York.

Geo. Martin Huss,
Architect,
New-York.

Six Mantels like this in the various offices.

side

Office Partition.

Front

Plan

Scale

W.C. &c, 2d. floor.

2d. floor

All the work shown is of selected Black Walnut, finished with dull hard oil finish. Alternate strips are reeded. Squares with turned reeds are of Santo Domingo Mahagony.

First Floor of Offices.

Office

Office

Hall

Office

Porch

Safe

W.C.

Scale

½ Landing

½ Landing

Window on Landing

Ventilator

W.C.

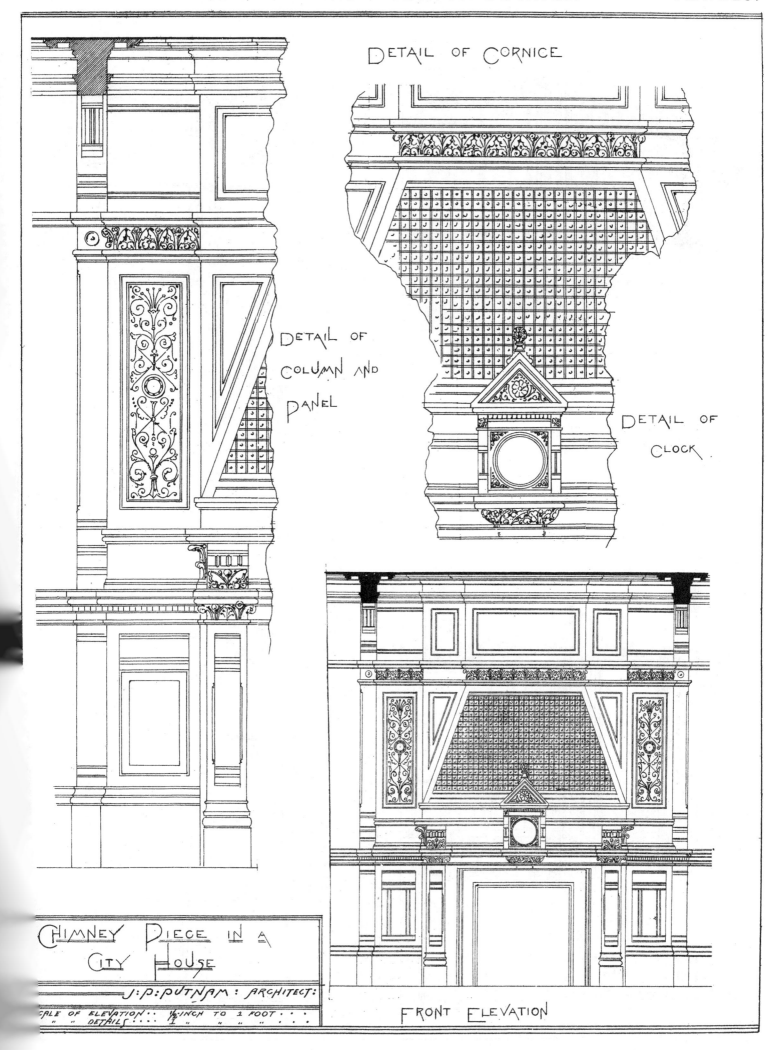

DETAIL OF CORNICE

DETAIL OF
COLUMN AND
PANEL

DETAIL OF
CLOCK

CHIMNEY PIECE IN A
CITY HOUSE

J: P: PUTNAM: ARCHITECT:

SCALE OF ELEVATION ·· ½ INCH TO 1 FOOT · · ·
     "   DETAILS · · · · · 1 "   "   "   · · · ·

FRONT ELEVATION

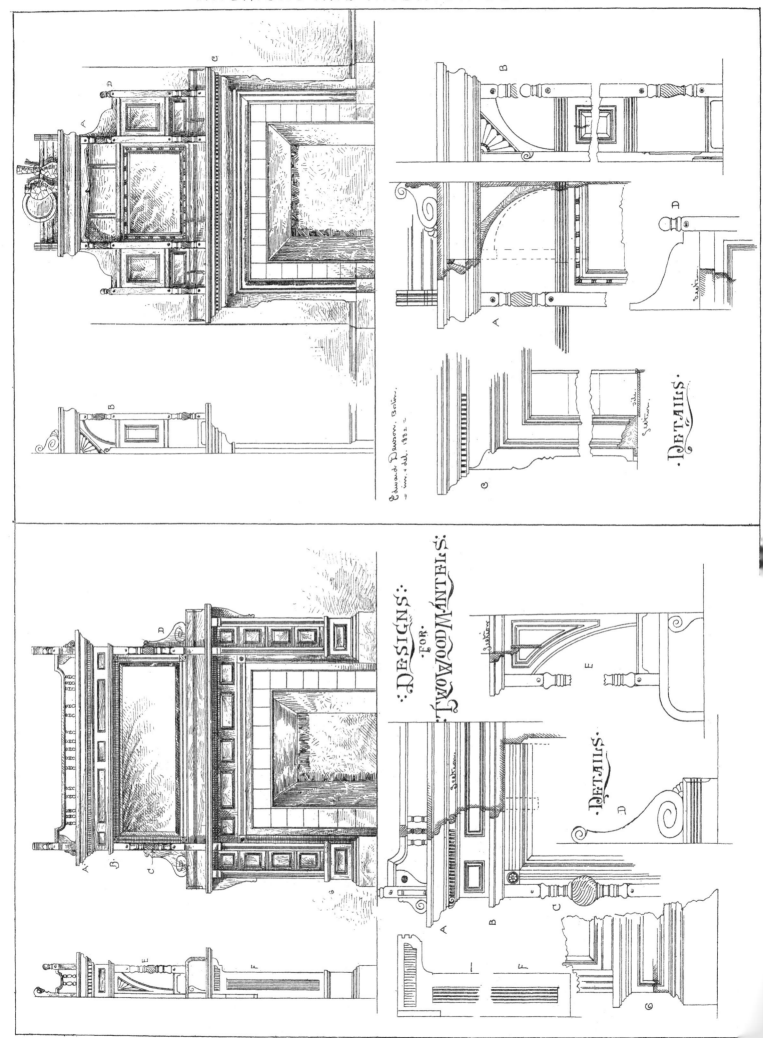

·DETAILS·

·DESIGNS· ·FOR· ·TWO·WOOD·MANTELS·

·DETAILS·

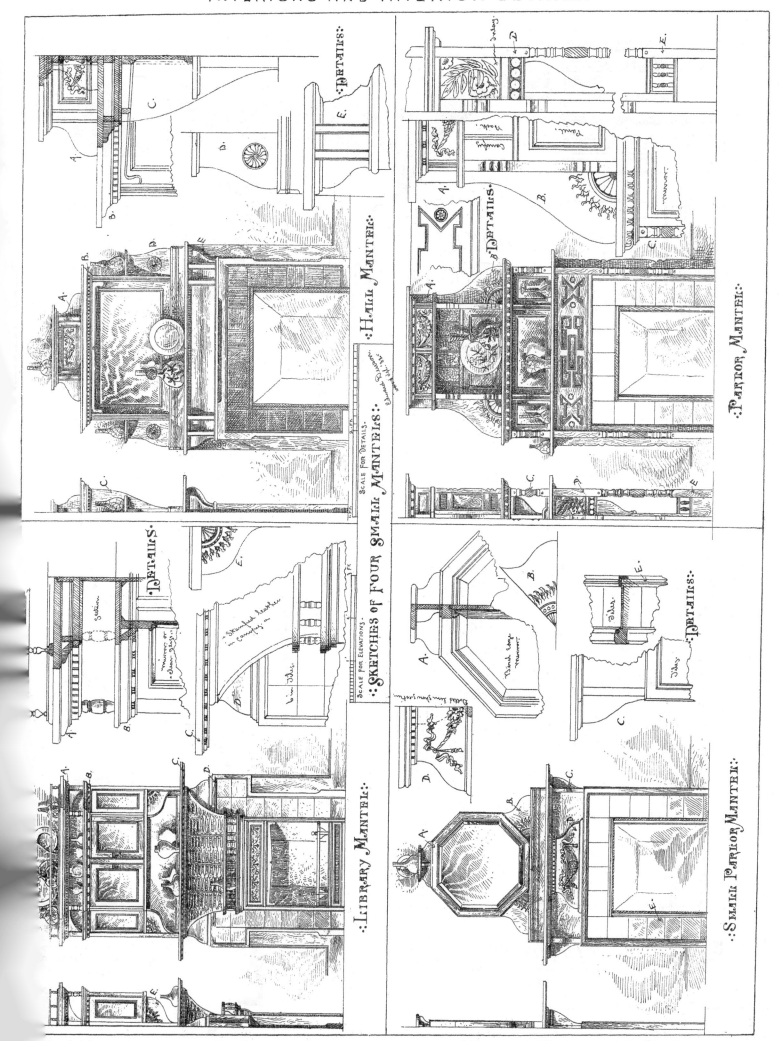

:·DETAILS:·

:·H·ALL MANTEL:·

:·PARLOR MANTEL:·

SCALE FOR DETAILS.

:·SKETCHES of FOUR SMALL MANTELS:·

SCALE FOR ELEVATIONS.

:·DETAILS:·

:·DETAILS:·

:·LIBRARY MANTEL:·

:·SMALL PARLOR MANTEL:·

Full Motto { Eat thy bread with joy. and drink thy wine with a merry heart. Ecc. IX. 7.

Section "A B" Tile

Eat Thy Bre And Drink Thy Wi Ecc.

E

D

TILES

A Corner Dining Room

Fire place opening 2:0" x 2: 7"

Brass frame

Tile hearth

shelf line

½ plan.

shelf.

grooves

Dentils

Panel "D"

center line

Mould at "E."

Base "C"

Mantel-piece

Rossiter and Wright.

The scale is One inch to one foot for general drawings and two thirds full size for Detail.

I

East Hames or West best

Art TILES

Brass frame

Fire place opening 1:8" wide 2:6" high.

iron back. Basket grate

Tile hearth

A sitting Mantel-Room piece

½ plan

Base block "H"

Section on line "F G"

cornice at "I"

Dentils

Moul aroun Motto panel

Edg of she

grooves

Mottoes engraved in the wood and picked out in co

shelf line

Tile.

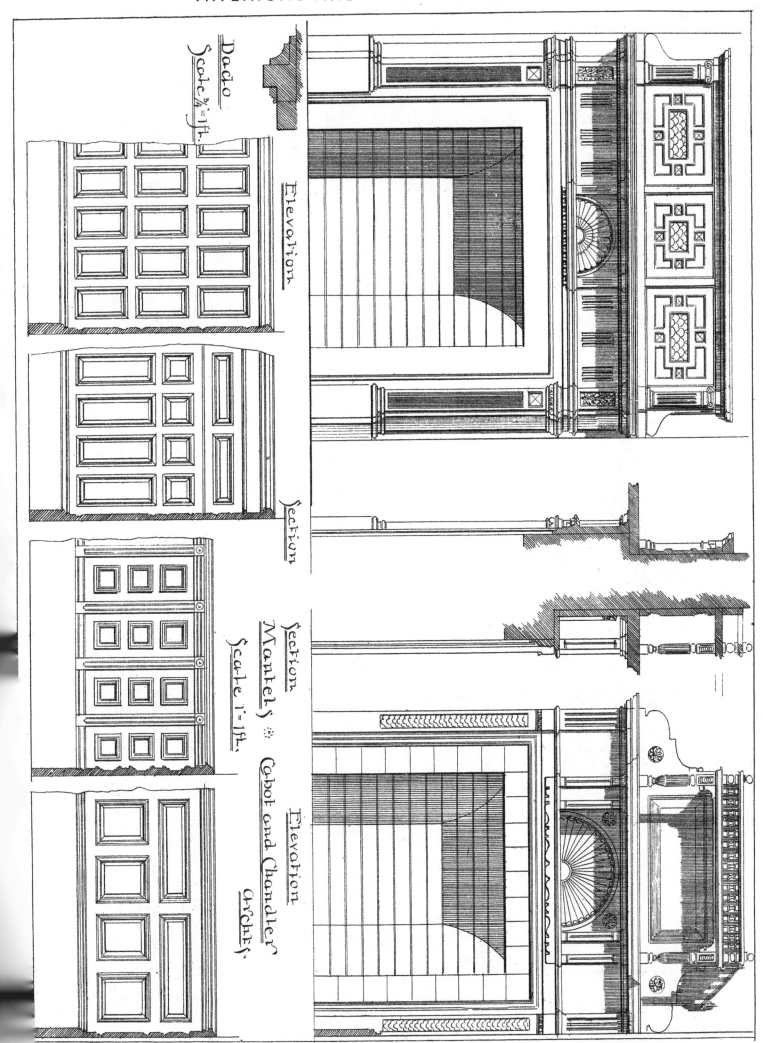

Dado
Scale ¾" = 1ft.

Elevation

Section

Section
Mantels
Scale 1" = 1ft.

Elevation

Cabot and Chandler
Archts.

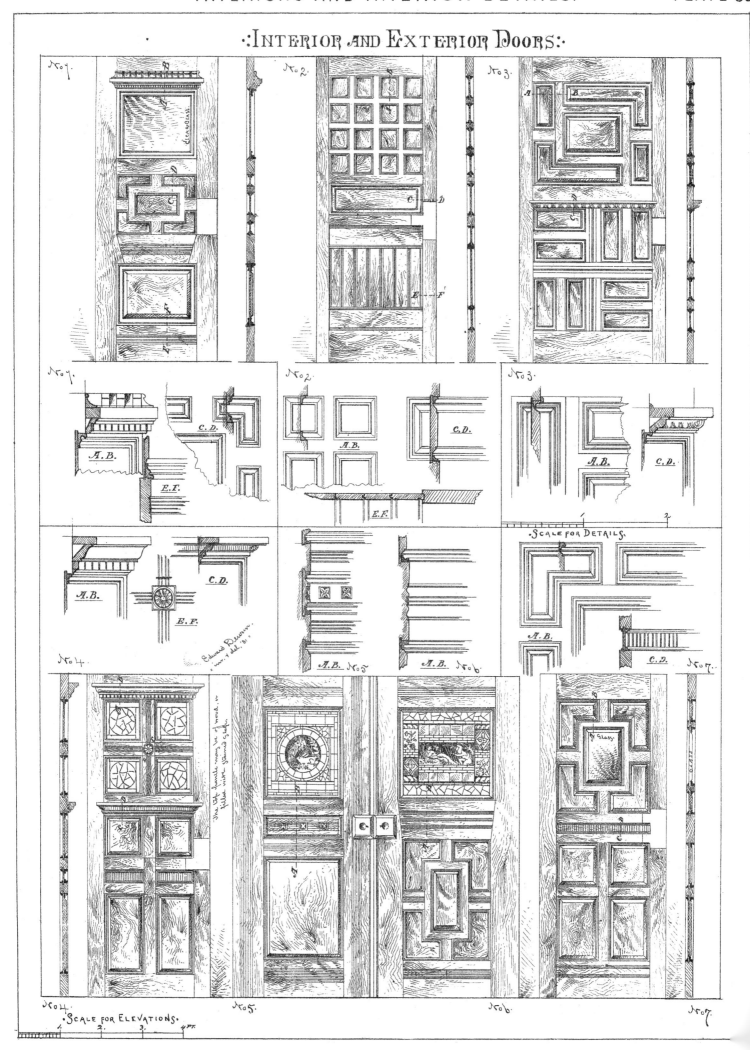

:INTERIOR AND EXTERIOR DOORS:·

·SCALE FOR DETAILS.

·SCALE FOR ELEVATIONS.

EXAMPLES
— OF —
WINDOW AND DOOR FINISH

SCALE OF ELEVATIONS. $\frac{1}{2}$ IN. = 1 FT.
SCALE OF DETAILS 1 IN. = 1 FT.

Gould & Angell.

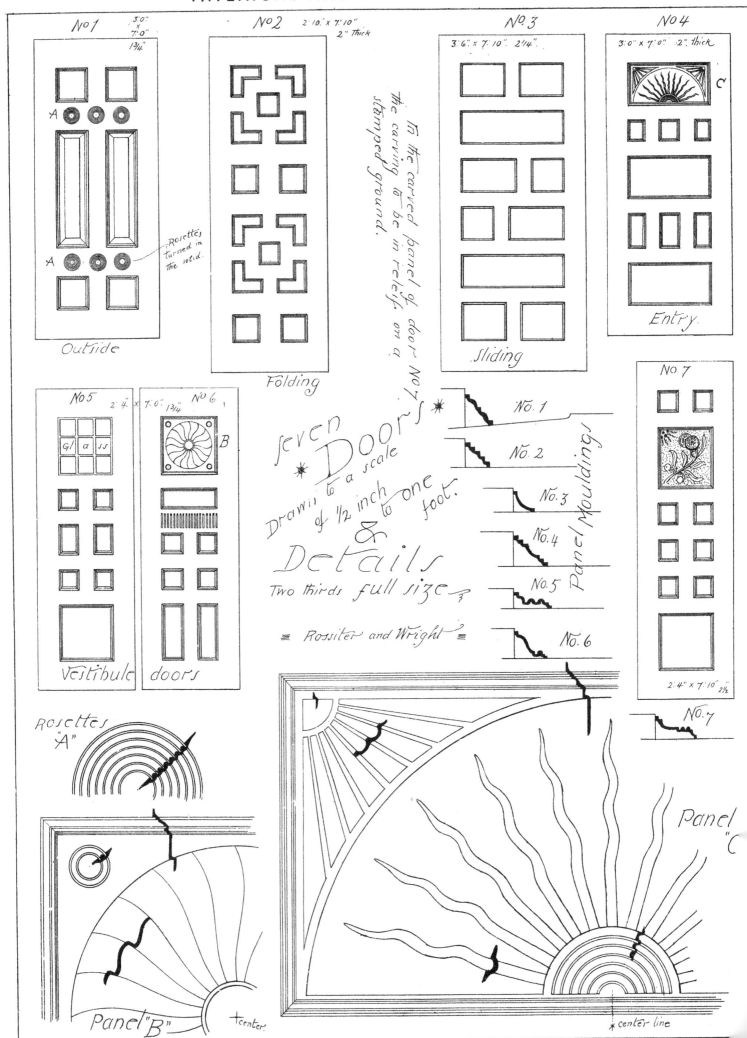

No 1

3'0" x 7'0" 1¾

A

A

Rosettes turned in the solid.

Outside

No 2

2'10" x 7'10" 2" Thick

Folding

No 3

3'6" x 7'10" 2¼".

Sliding

No 4

3'0" x 7'0" 2" thick

C

Entry.

No 5

2'4" x 7'0" 1¾

Glass

No 6

B

Vestibule doors

In the carved panel of door No 7 the carving to be in relief, on a stamped ground.

Seven Doors Drawn to a scale of ½ inch to one foot. & Details Two thirds full size

Rossiter and Wright

No. 1
No. 2
No. 3
No. 4
No. 5
No. 6

Panel Moulding

No. 7

No 7

2'4" x 7'10" 2½

Rosettes "A"

Panel "B"

+ center

Panel "C

* center line

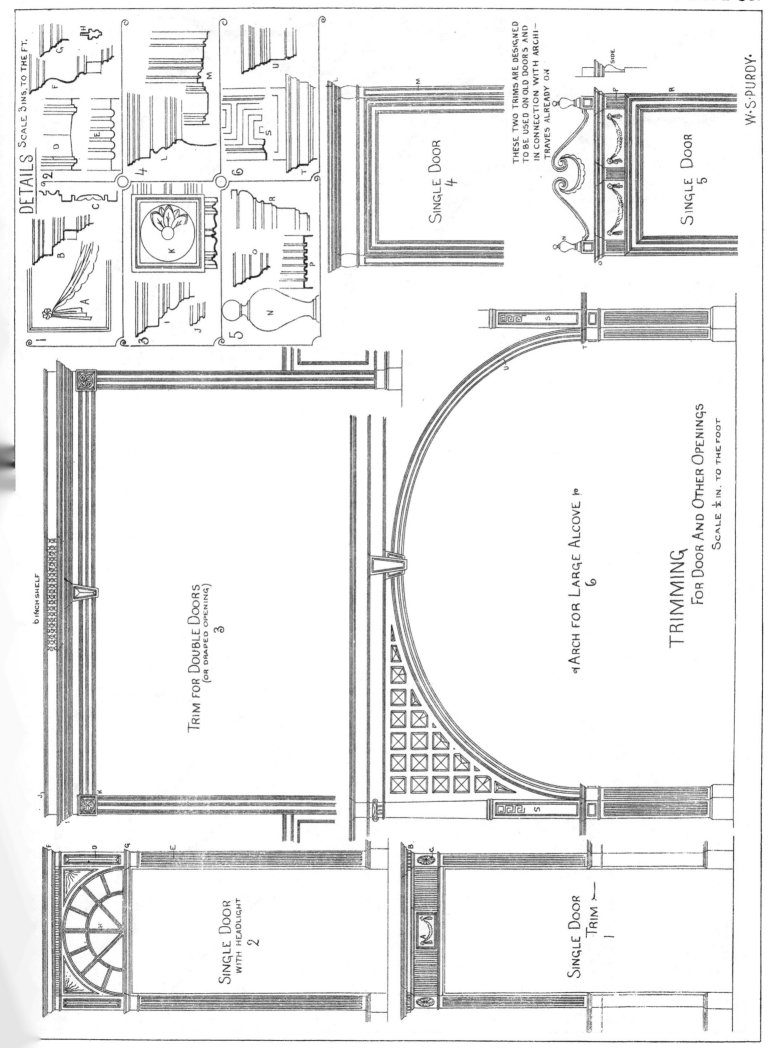

DETAILS SCALE 3 INS. TO THE FT.

SINGLE DOOR 4

THESE TWO TRIMS ARE DESIGNED TO BE USED ON OLD DOORS AND IN CONNECTION WITH ARCHI— TRAVES ALREADY ON

SINGLE DOOR 5

W·S·PURDY.

BIRCH SHELF

TRIM FOR DOUBLE DOORS (OR DRAPED OPENING) 3

ARCH FOR LARGE ALCOVE 6

TRIMMING FOR DOOR AND OTHER OPENINGS
SCALE ½ IN. TO THE FOOT

SINGLE DOOR WITH HEADLIGHT 2

SINGLE DOOR TRIM 1

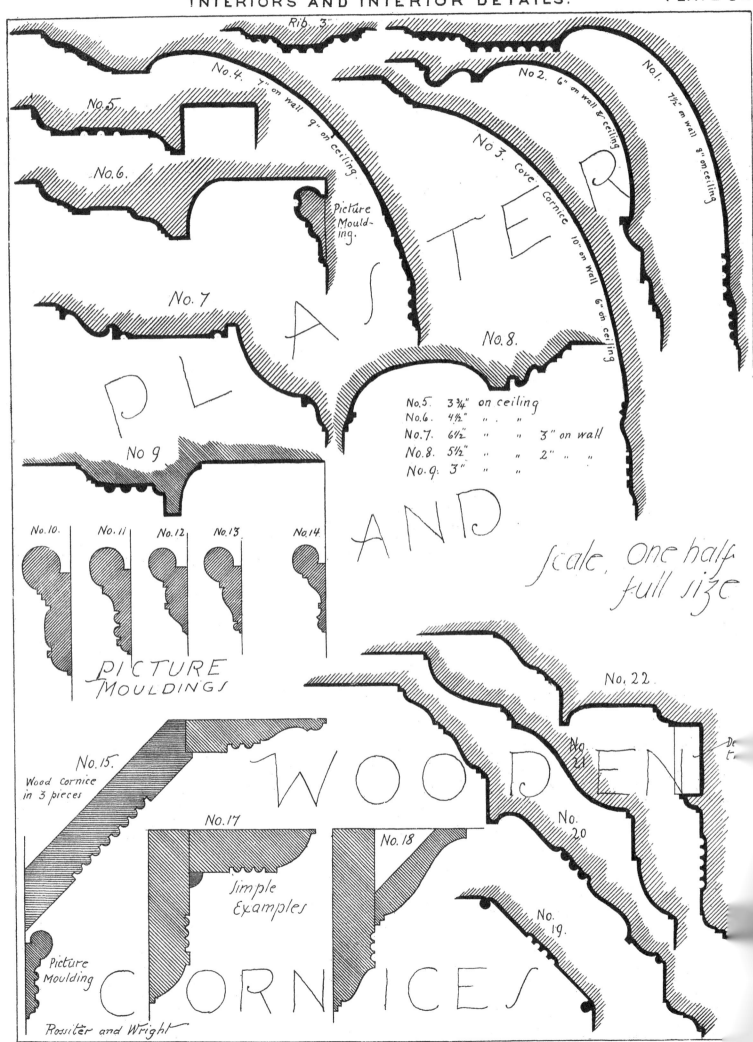

Rib. 3"

No.4. 7" on wall 9" on ceiling

No.5

No.6.

No. 2. 6" on wall & ceiling

No.1. 7½" on wall 8" on ceiling

No.3. Cove Cornice 10" on wall 6" on ceiling

PLASTER

Picture Moulding.

No. 7

No.8.

No 9

No.5. 3¾" on ceiling
No.6. 4½"   "   "
No.7. 6½"   "   "   3" on wall
No.8. 5½"   "   "   2" "   "
No.9. 3"   "   "

AND

No. 10. No. 11. No. 12. No. 13. No. 14.

PICTURE MOULDINGS

Scale, one half full size

No. 22.

No. 21

No. 20

No. 15.

Wood cornice in 3 pieces

No. 17

No. 18

WOODEN

Simple Examples

No. 19.

Picture Moulding

CORNICES

Rossiter and Wright

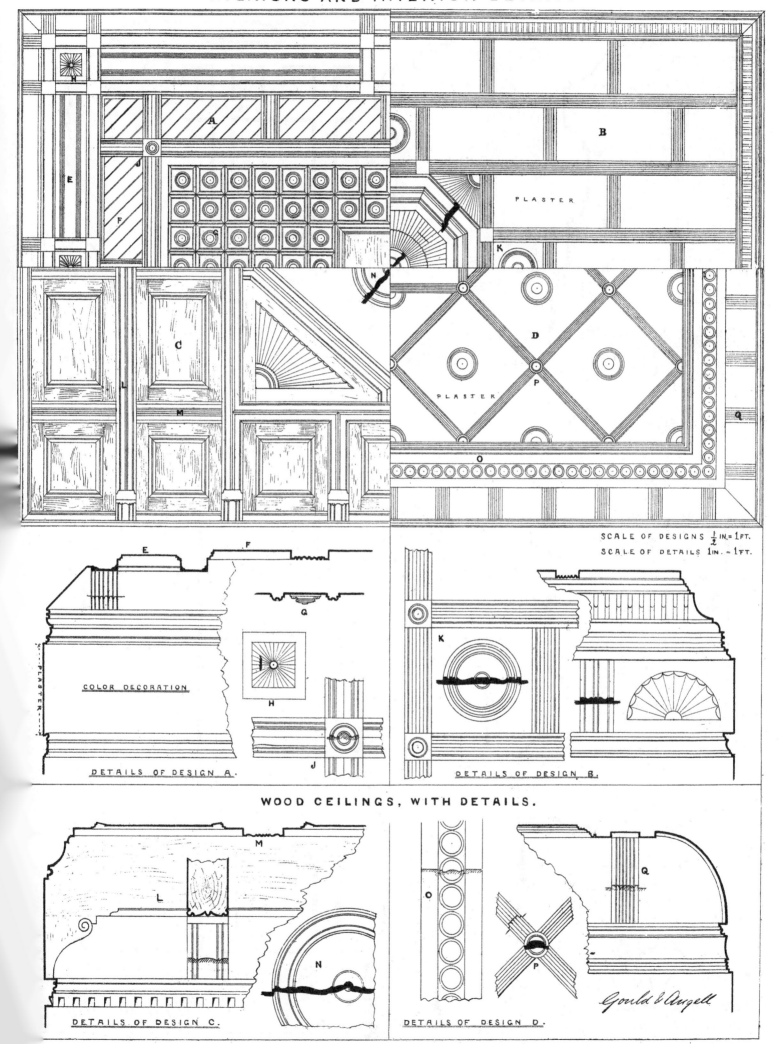

SCALE OF DESIGNS ½ IN.= 1FT.
SCALE OF DETAILS 1IN. = 1FT.

COLOR DECORATION

DETAILS OF DESIGN A.

DETAILS OF DESIGN B.

WOOD CEILINGS, WITH DETAILS.

DETAILS OF DESIGN C.

DETAILS OF DESIGN D.

Gould & Angell

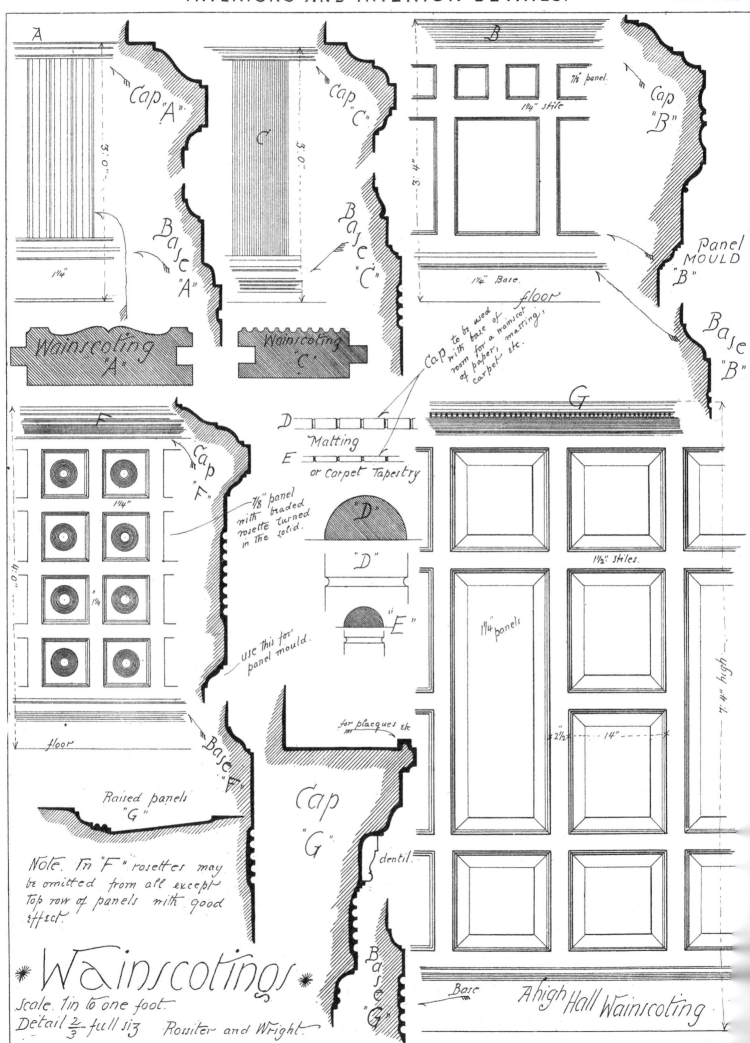

A

Cap "A".

Base "A"

3.0"

1¼"

Wainscoting "A"

C

Cap "C"

Base "C"

3.0"

Wainscoting "C"

B

7/8" panel.

1¼" stile

Cap "B"

1¼" Base.

floor

Panel MOULD "B"

Base "B"

Cap to be used with base of room for a wainscot of paper, matting, carpet etc.

F

Cap "F"

1¼"

1¼"

4.0"

floor

Base "F"

Raised panels "G"

D

Matting

E

or Carpet Tapestry

7/8" panel with braded rosette turned in the solid.

"D"

"D"

"E"

use this for panel mould.

for plaques etc

Cap "G"

dentil.

G

1½" stiles.

1¼" panels

2½" · 14"

7 ft. 4 high

Base "G"

Base

A high Hall Wainscoting

Note. In "F" rosettes may be omitted from all except top row of panels with good effect.

Wainscotings

Scale. 1 in to one foot.
Detail ⅔ full siz   Rossiter and Wright.

EXAMPLES OF PANELING ○○○ SCALES. ½ IN = 1 FT FOR ELEVATIONS 1 IN = 1 FT " DETAILS ○○○ Gould & Angell ○

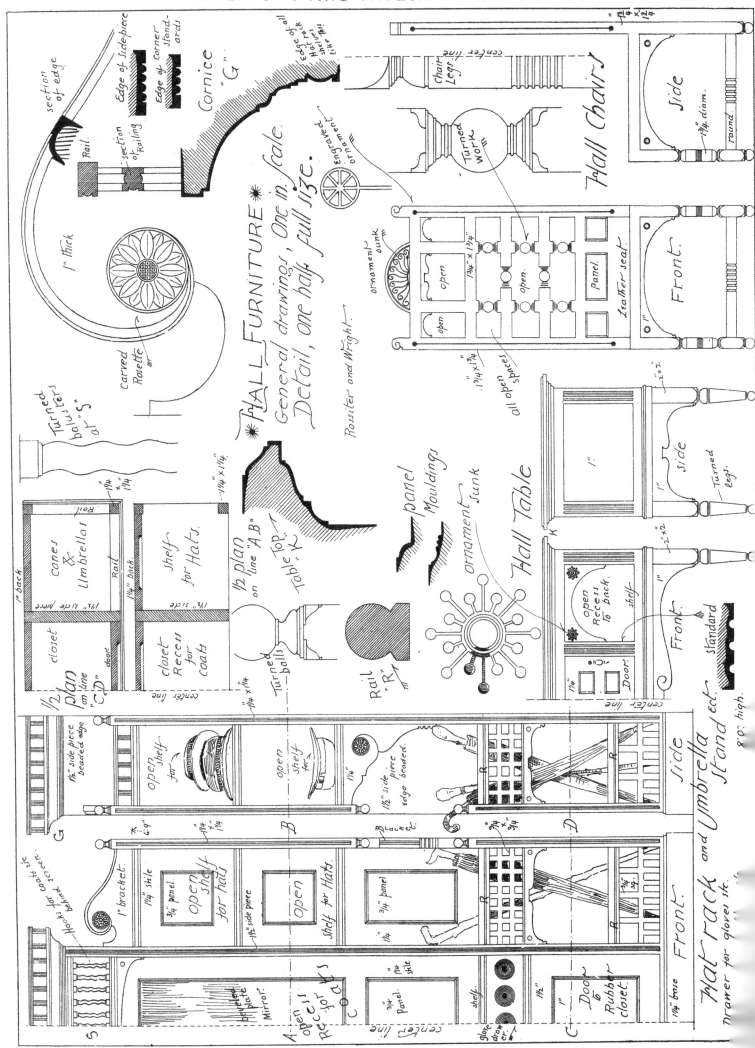

Hall Furniture
General drawings, One in. scale.
Detail, one half full size.

Rossiter and Wright.

Hall Chairs

Hall Table

Hat Rack and *Umbrella Stand* etc.

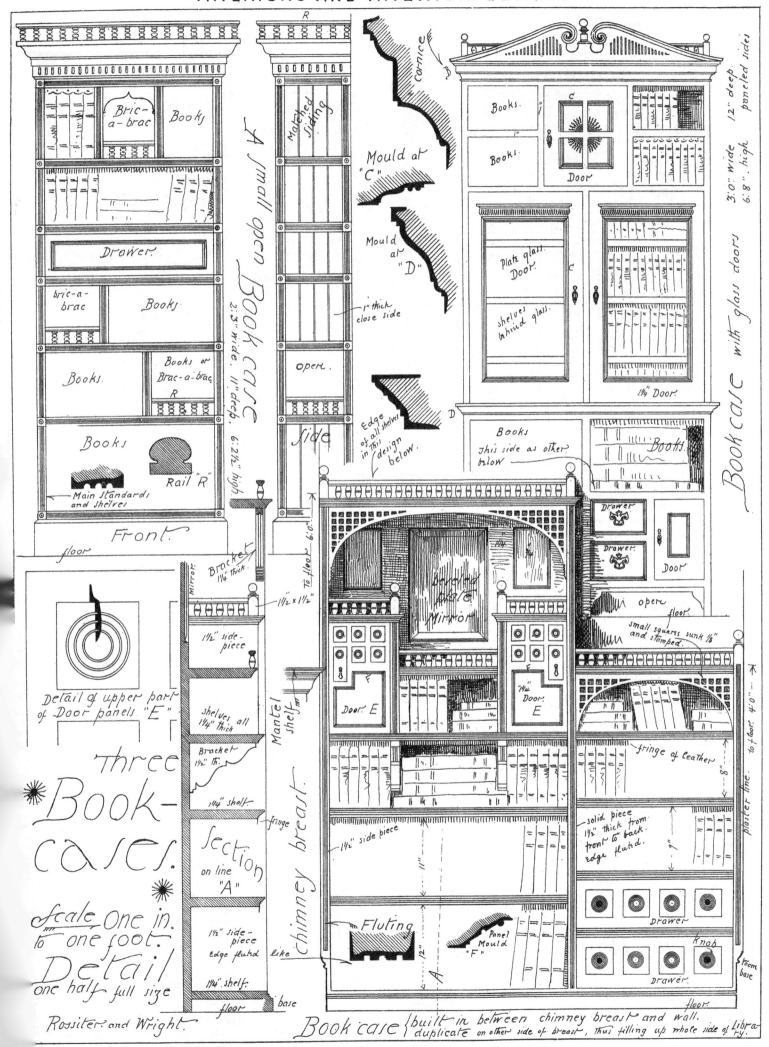

A small open Bookcase
2'3" wide, 11" deep, 6'2½" high.

Bric-a-brac Books

Drawer.

bric-a-brac Books

Books Books or Brac-a-brac R

Books Rail "R"

Main Standards and Shelves

Front.

floor

Matched siding

open.

side

cornice

Mould at "C"
1" thick close side

Mould at "D"

Edge of all shelves in this design below.

Book case with glass doors 3'0" wide 6'8". high 12" deep paneled sides

Books.

Books.

Door C

Plate glass Door.

shelves behind glass.

C

1¼" Door.

Books This side as other below Books

Drawer

Drawer

Door

open

small squares sunk ⅛" and stamped.

beveled plate Mirror

Door E 1¼" Door. E

fringe of leather 8"

1½" side piece

solid piece 1½" thick from front to back, edge fluted.

9"

11"

Fluting 12" A

Panel Mould "F"

Drawer Knob

Drawer

room base

floor

plaster line. to floor 4'0"

Mantel shelf

chimney breast.

like

fringe

1¼" shelf.

1½" side-piece edge fluted

1¼". shelf.

floor base

To floor 6'0"

Bracket 1¼" thick

1½" x 1½"

Mirror

1½" side-piece

shelves, all 1¼" thick

Bracket 1½" th.

Detail of upper part of Door panels "E".

three Book-cases.

scale one in. to one foot. Detail one half full size

Rossiter and Wright.

Section on line "A"

Book case {built in between chimney breast and wall.
duplicate on other side of breast, thus filling up whole side of Library.

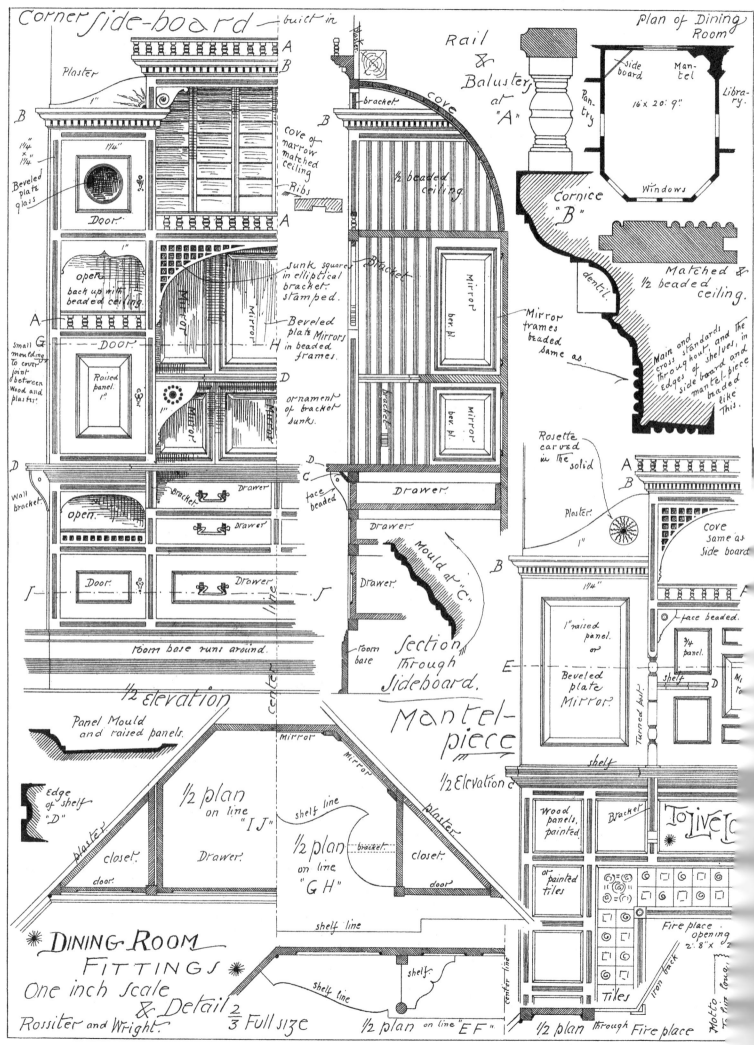

Corner Side-board — built in

Plan of Dining Room

Rail & Baluster at "A"

Cornice "B"

Matched & 1/2 beaded ceiling.

Main and cross standards throughout, and the edges of shelves, in side board and mantel-piece beaded like This.

Plaster

Beveled plate glass

Door.

open back up with beaded ceiling.

Small moulding to cover joint between wood and plaster.

Raised panel. 1"

Door.

Wall bracket.

open.

Door.

Drawer

Drawer

Drawer

Room base runs around.

1/2 Elevation

Panel Mould and raised panels.

Edge of shelf "D"

1/2 plan on line "I J"

Drawer

closet. door.

DINING-ROOM
FITTINGS
One inch Scale
& Detail 2/3 Full Size
Rossiter and Wright.

cove of narrow matched ceiling. Ribs

sunk square in elliptical bracket stamped.

Beveled plate Mirrors in beaded frames.

ornament of bracket sunk.

Mirror

Bracket

Mirror

Mirror

Bracket

face beaded

Drawer

Drawer

Drawer

room base

Mould at "C"

Section Through Sideboard.

Mantel-piece

1/2 Elevation

1/2 plan on line "G H"

closet. door.

shelf line

1/2 plan on line "E F"

1/2 beaded ceiling

Mirror bev. pl.

Mirror bev. pl.

Mirror frames beaded same as

dentil.

Rosette carved in the solid

Plaster 1"

cove same as Side board

1" raised panel. or Beveled plate Mirror.

face beaded.

3/4 panel.

shelf

Turned post.

shelf

Wood panels, painted or painted tiles

Bracket

To Live L...

Tiles

Iron back

Fire place opening 2'.8" x 2

1/2 plan through Fire place

Motto...

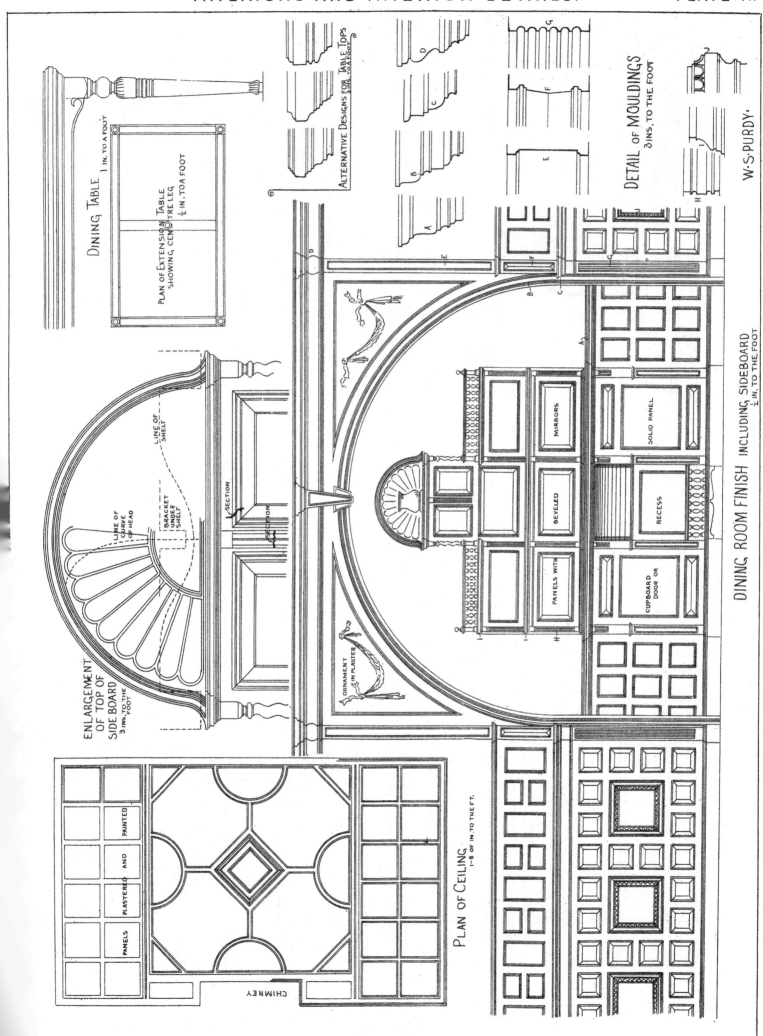

DINING TABLE 1 IN. TO A FOOT

PLAN OF EXTENSION TABLE SHOWING CENTRE LEG. ¼ IN. TO A FOOT

ALTERNATIVE DESIGNS FOR TABLE TOPS 3 INS. TO A FOOT

DETAIL of MOULDINGS 3 INS. TO THE FOOT

W·S·PURDY.

ENLARGEMENT OF TOP OF SIDE BOARD 3 INS. TO THE FOOT

LINE OF CURVE OF HEAD

LINE OF SHELF

BRACKET UNDER SHELF

SECTION

ORNAMENT ¾ IN PLASTER

MIRRORS

BEVELED

SOLID PANEL

PANELS WITH

RECESS

CUPBOARD DOOR OR

DINING ROOM FINISH INCLUDING SIDEBOARD ½ IN. TO THE FOOT

PANELS PLASTERED AND PAINTED

CHIMNEY

PLAN OF CEILING 1-8 OF IN. TO THE FT.

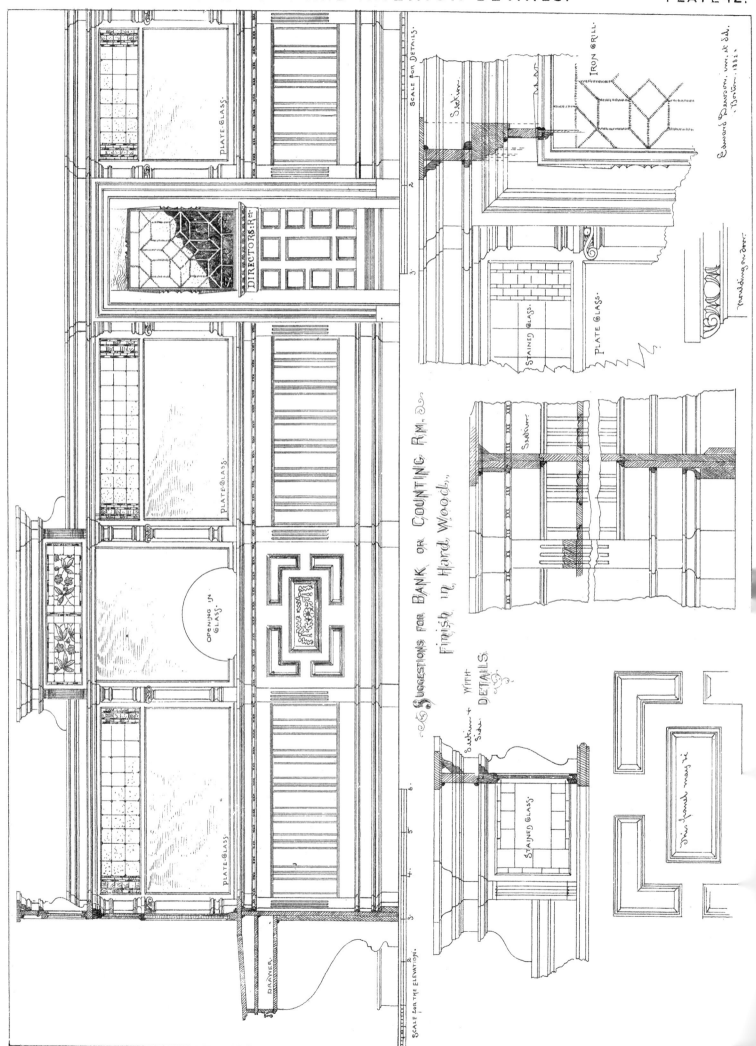

Suggestions for Bank or Counting Rm.
Finish in Hard Wood.
Section with Side Details.

PLATE GLASS.

DIRECTORS RM

PLATE GLASS

OPENING IN GLASS

PLATE GLASS

PLATE GLASS

DRAWER

SCALE FOR THE ELEVATION.

SCALE FOR DETAILS.

IRON GRILL.

STAINED GLASS.

PLATE GLASS.

STAINED GLASS.

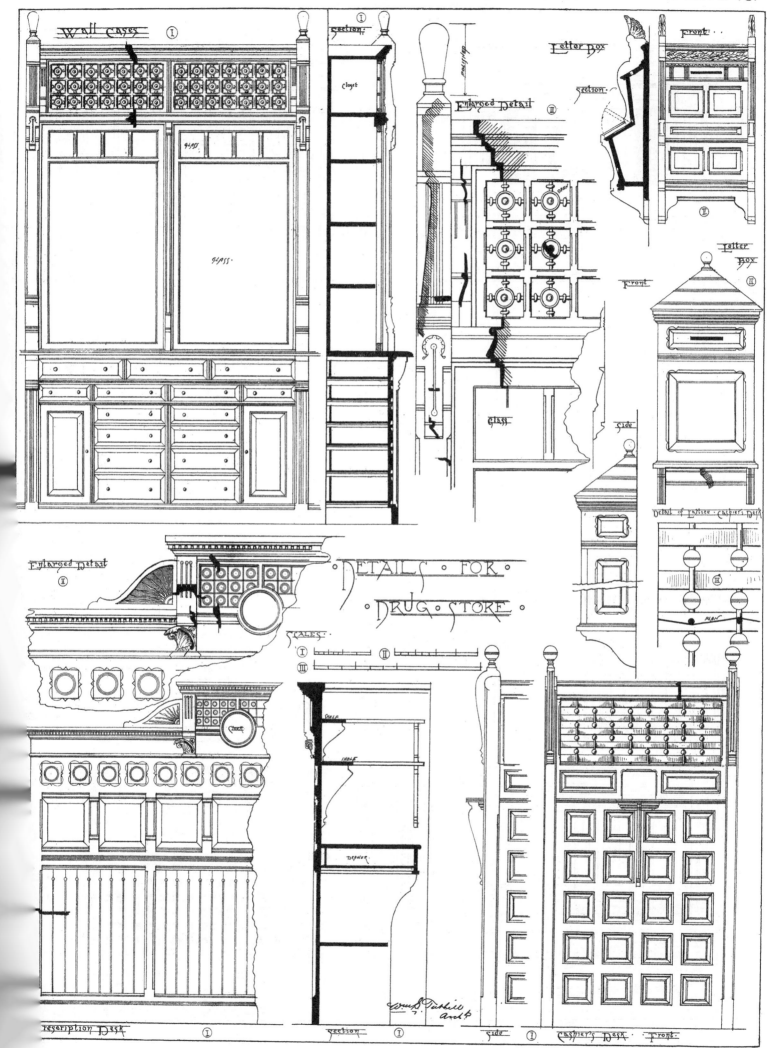

Wall Cases

Section

Letter Box

Front

Enlarged Detail

Closet

Glass

Glass

Letter Box

Front

Side

Detail of Lattice Cashier's Desk

Enlarged Detail

Details for Drug Store

Scales

Shelf

Table

Drawer

Plan

Prescription Desk

Section

Side

Cashier's Desk Front.

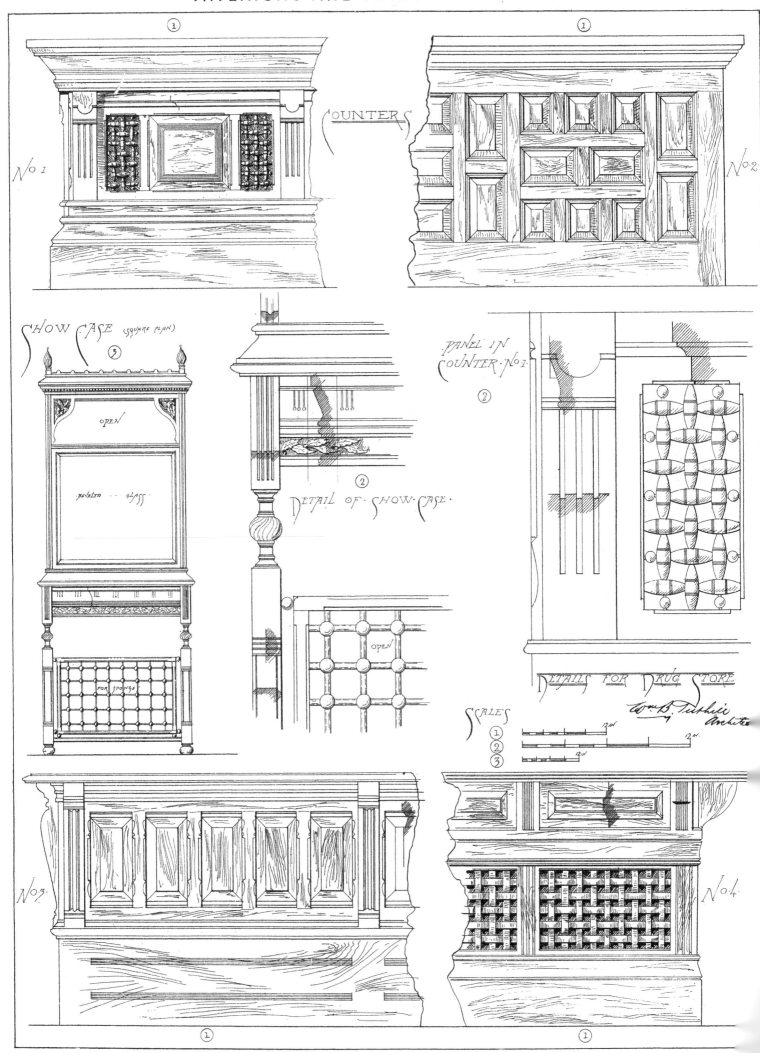

COUNTERS

No 1

No 2

SHOW CASE (SQUARE PLAN)

OPEN

BEVELED GLASS

FOR SPONGE

DETAIL OF SHOW CASE.

OPEN

PANEL IN COUNTER No 1.

DETAILS FOR DRUG STORE

SCALES

Wm B. Tuthill
Architect

No 3

No 4

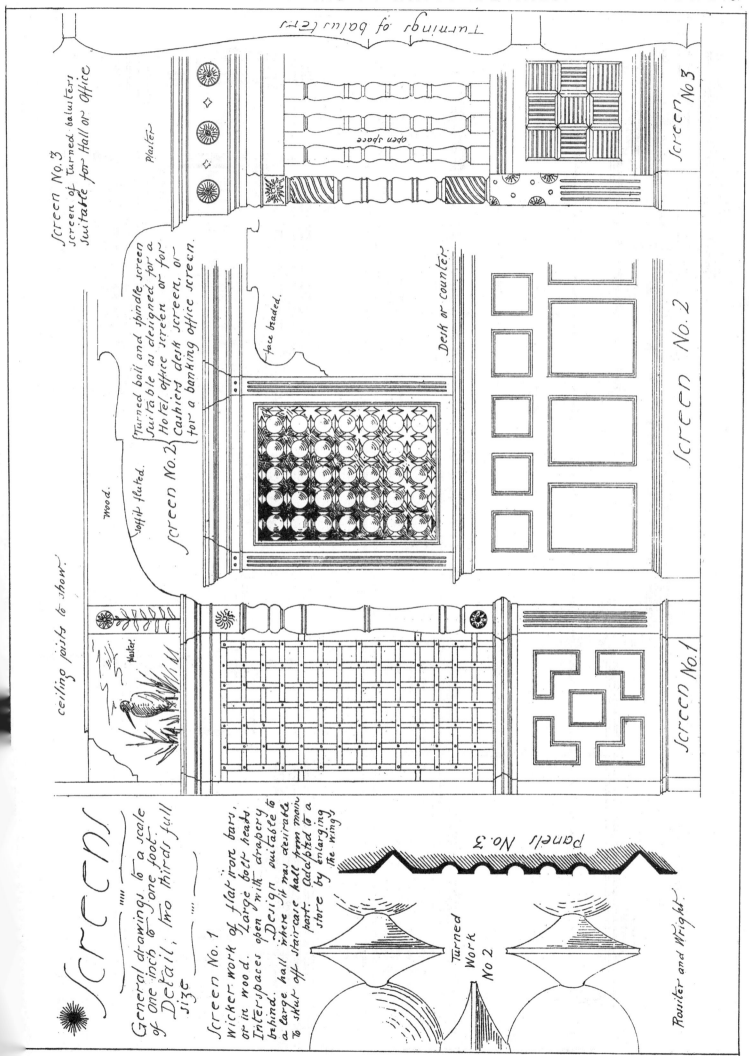

Turnings of balusters

Screen No. 3
Screen of turned balusters
Suitable for Hall or Office

Plaster

open space

Screen No. 3

Screen No. 2
Turned ball and spindle screen
Suitable as designed for a
Hotel office screen or for
Cashier's desk screen, or
for a banking office screen.

face beaded.

Desk or counter

wood.

soffit fluted.

Screen No. 2

Screen No. 2

ceiling joists to show.

Plaster.

Screen No. 1

Screen No. 1

Screens

General drawings to a scale
of one inch to one foot.
Detail, two thirds full
size

Screen No. 1
Wicker-work of flat iron bars,
or in wood. Large bolt heads.
Interspaces open with drapery
behind. Design suitable to
a large hall where it may desirable
to shut off staircase hall from main
part. Adapted to a
store by enlarging
the wings

Panel No. 3

Turned
Work
No 2

Rossiter and Wright.

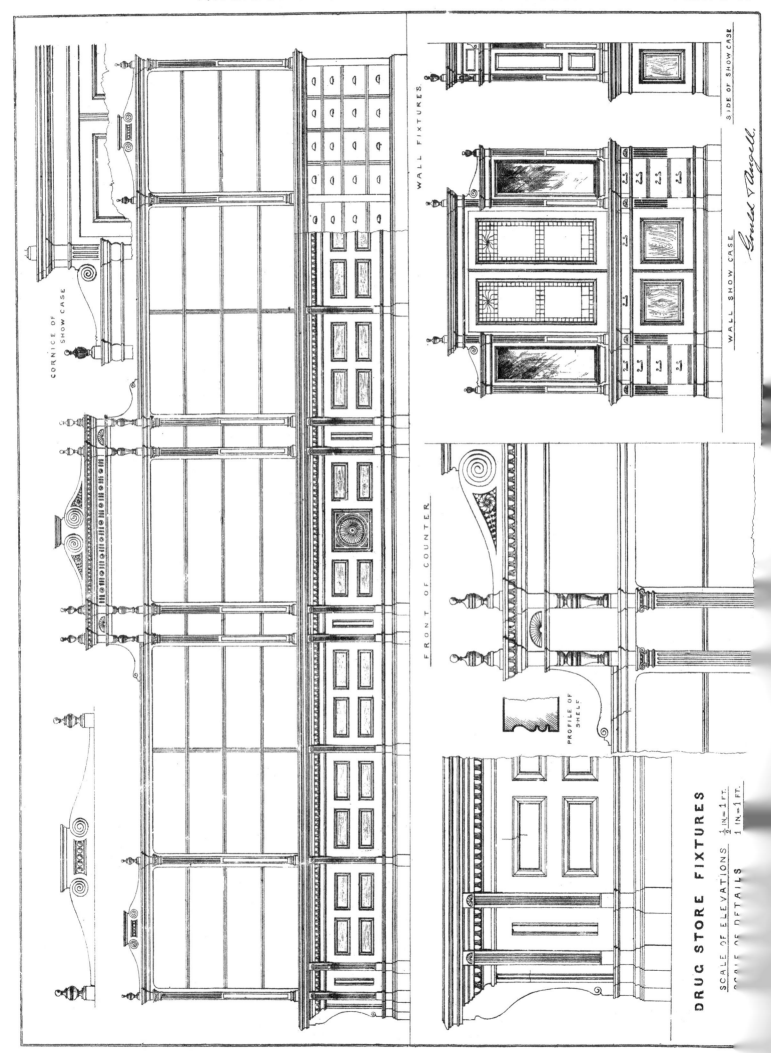

CORNICE OF SHOW CASE

WALL FIXTURES

SIDE OF SHOW CASE

WALL SHOW CASE

FRONT OF COUNTER

PROFILE OF SHELF

DRUG STORE FIXTURES

SCALE OF ELEVATIONS $\frac{1}{4}$ IN. = 1 FT.

$\frac{1}{2}$ IN. = 1 FT.

1 IN. = 1 FT.

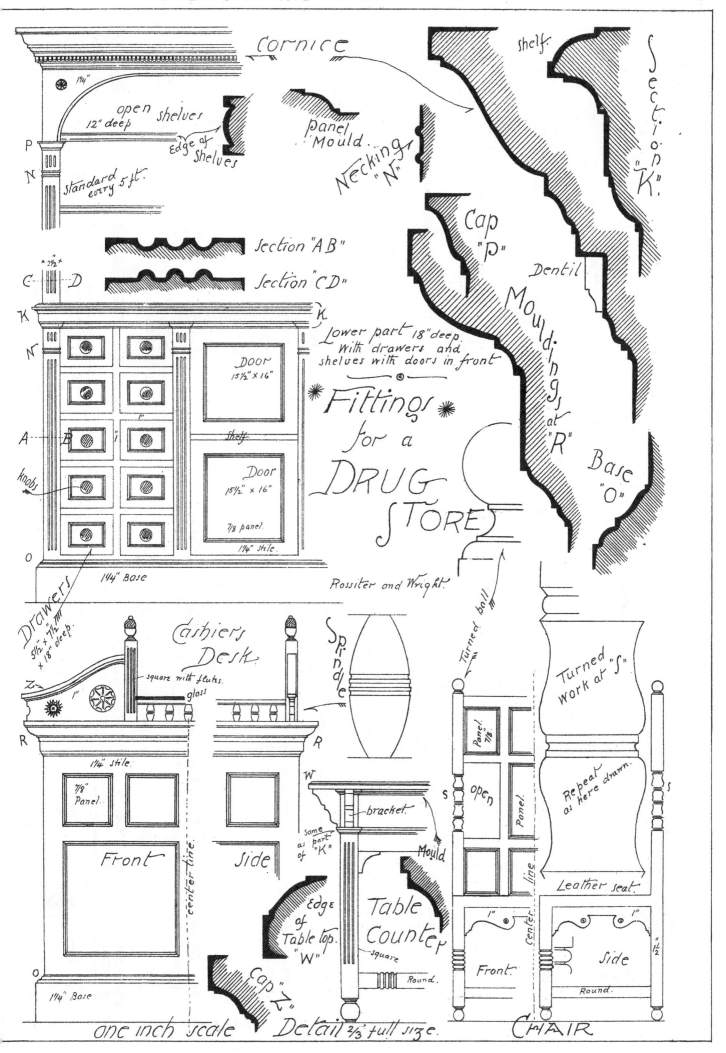

Cornice

open shelves
12" deep

Edge of
Shelves

Standard
every 5 ft.

Panel
Mould.

Necking "N"

shelf.

Section "K"

Cap "P"

Dentil

Moulding at "R"

Base "O"

Section "AB"

Section "CD"

Lower part 18" deep.
With drawers and
shelves with doors in front

Door
15½" × 16"

shelf

Door
15½" × 16"

7/8 panel.

1¼" stile.

knobs

* Fittings *
for a
DRUG
STORE

Rossiter and Wright.

1¼" Base

Drawers
5½" × 7½"
× 18" deep.

Cashiers
Desk

square with flutes.
glass

Spindle

Turned ball

Turned
work at "S"

Repeat
as here drawn.

1¼" stile.

7/8"
Panel.

Front

Side

center line

bracket.

Same
as part
of "K"

Edge
of
Table top
"W"

Table
Counter

square

Round.

Mould.

Panel.
7/8

open

Panel.

Leather seat.

1"   1"

Front.   Side

center line

1½

Round.

CHAIR

1¼" Base

one inch scale

Detail ⅔ full size.

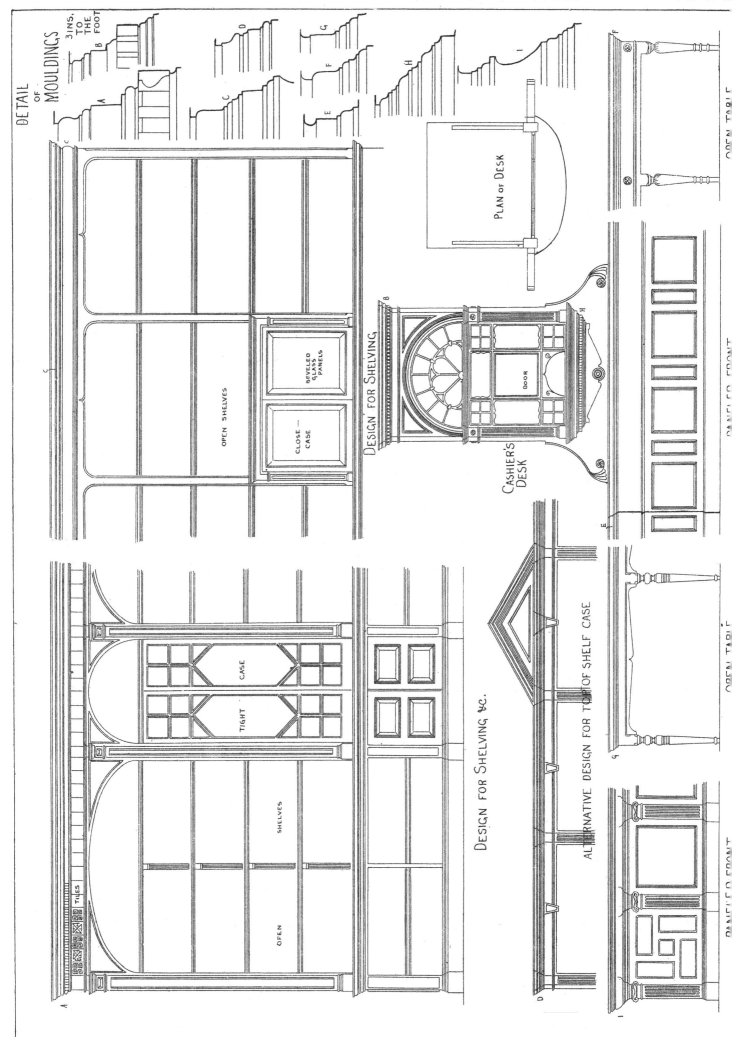

DETAIL OF MOULDINGS

3 INS. TO THE FOOT

OPEN SHELVES

BEVELED GLASS PANELS

CLOSE CASE

DESIGN FOR SHELVING

PLAN OF DESK

CASHIER'S DESK

DOOR

TILES

TIGHT CASE

SHELVES

OPEN

DESIGN FOR SHELVING &c.

ALTERNATIVE DESIGN FOR TOP OF SHELF CASE

OPEN TABLE

PANELED FRONT

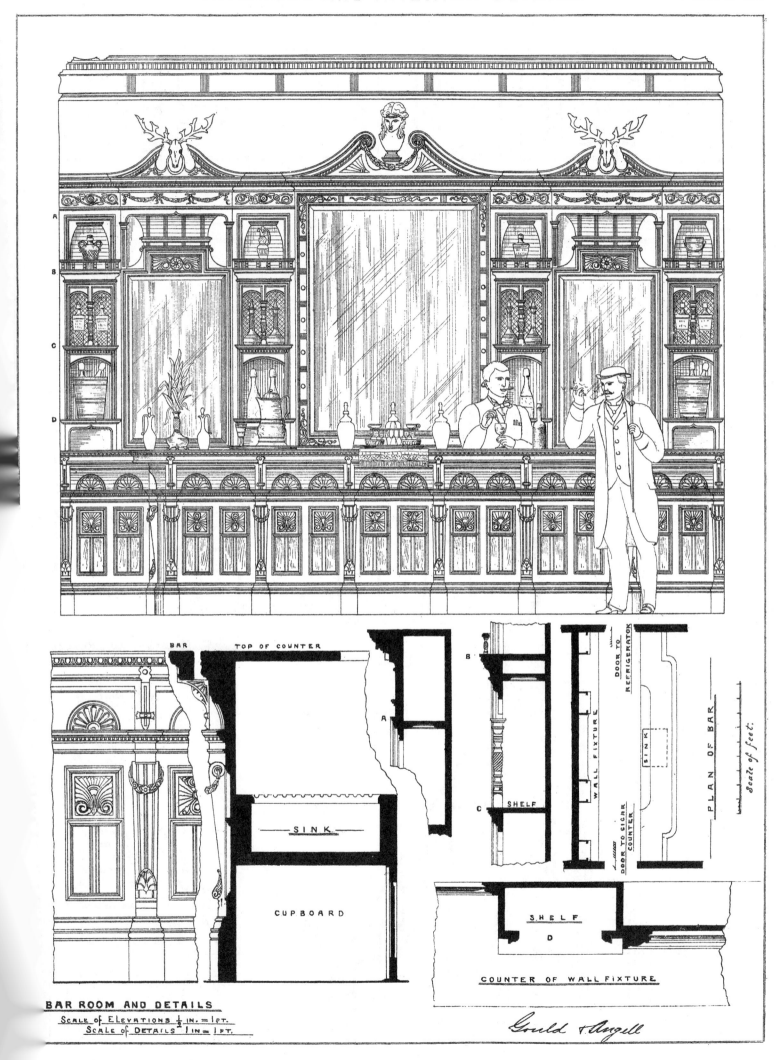

BAR　TOP OF COUNTER

SINK

CUPBOARD

DOOR TO REFRIGERATOR

WALL FIXTURE

SINK

DOOR TO SIGN COUNTER

SHELF

PLAN OF BAR

Scale of feet.

SHELF

D

COUNTER OF WALL FIXTURE

BAR ROOM AND DETAILS

Scale of Elevations ½ In. = 1 Ft.
Scale of Details 1 In. = 1 Ft.

Gould & Angell

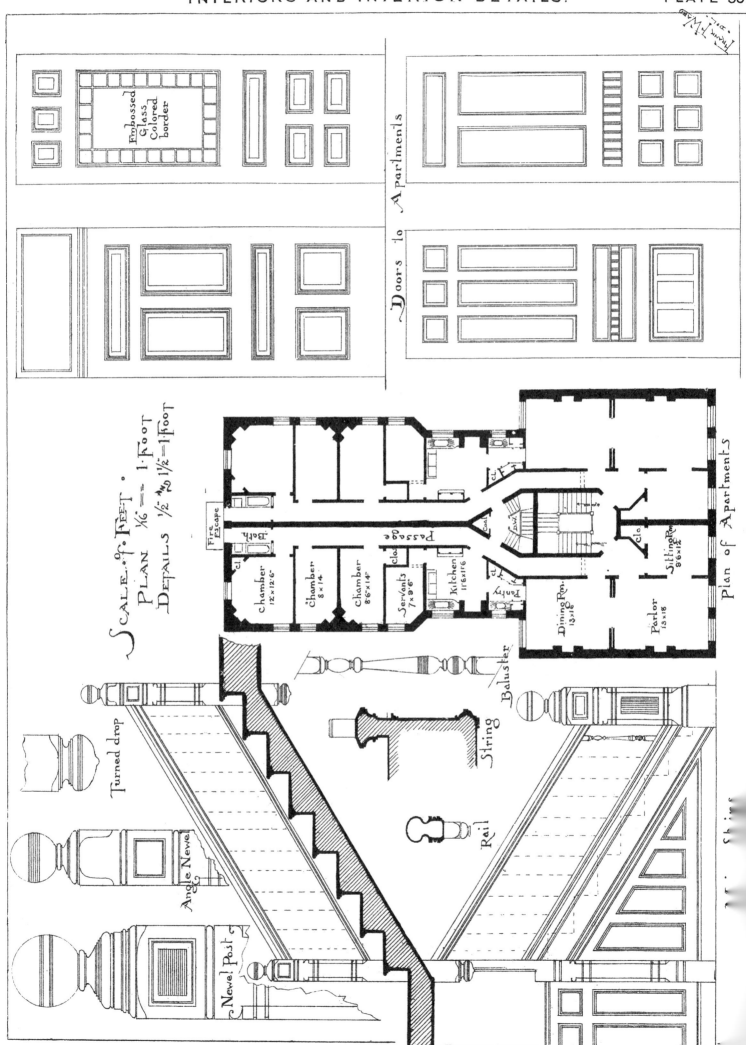

Embossed Glass Colored border

Doors to Apartments

Scale of Feet.
Plan ½" = 1·Foot
Details ½" and 1½" = 1·Foot

Fire Escape

Bath

Chamber 12×12·6"

Chamber 8×14

Chamber 8·6×14

Servants 7×9·6"

Closet

Passage

Kitchen 11·6×11·6

Pantry

Dining Rm. 13×16

Parlor 13×16

Sitting Rm 9·6×12

Cl.

Clo.

Plan of Apartments

Turned drop

Angle Newel

Newel Post

Baluster

String

Rail

Stairs

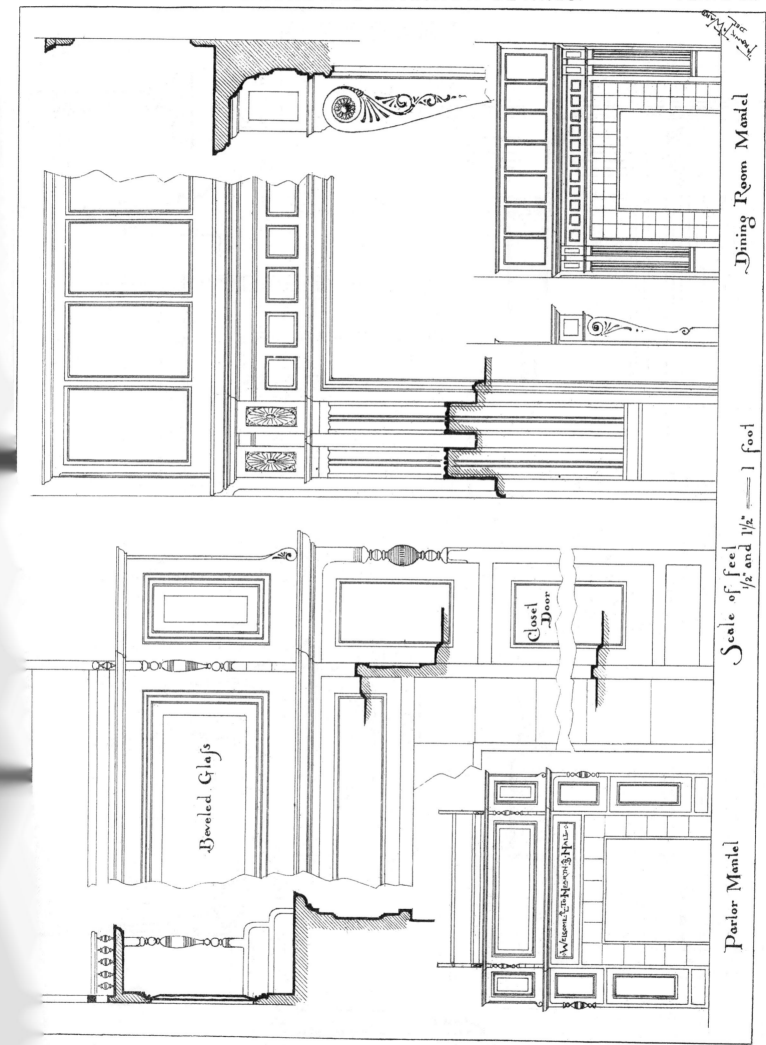

Dining Room Mantel

Parlor Mantel

Scale of feet ½" and 1½" = 1 foot

Beveled Glass

Closet Door

WELCOME·TO·NEARGH·@·HALL·

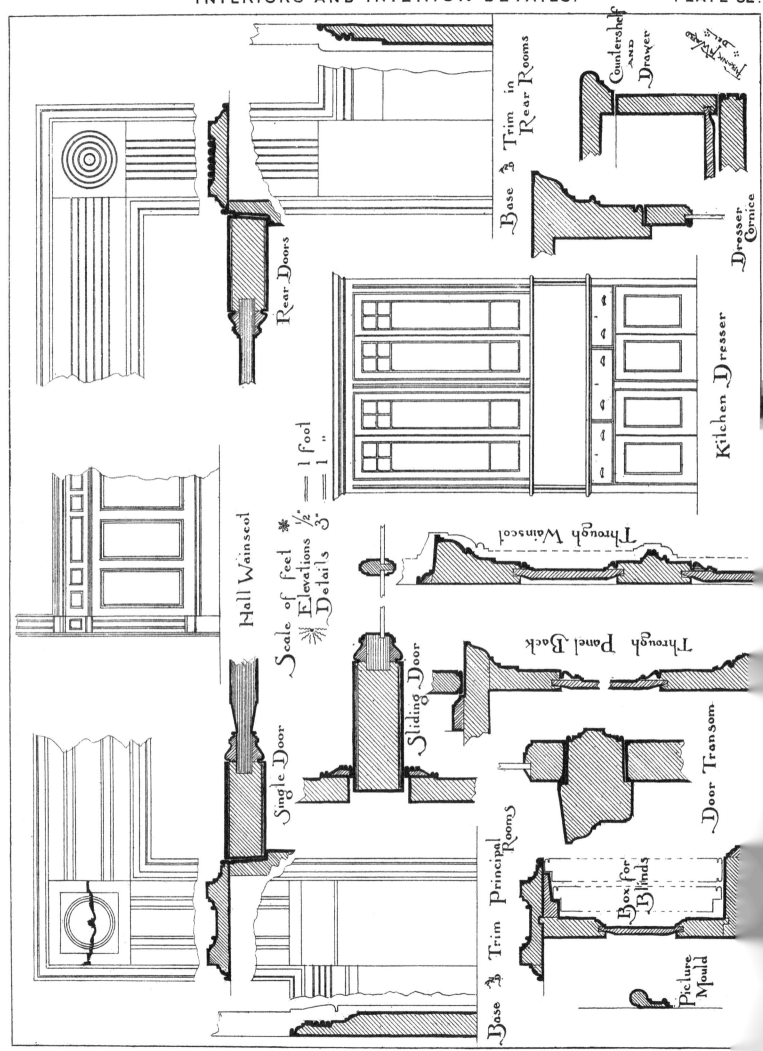

Base & Trim in Rear Rooms

Countershelf and Drawer

Frank T. Bell Del.

Rear Doors

Dresser Cornice

Kitchen Dresser

Hall Wainscot

Scale of feet
Elevations ½" = 1 Foot
Details 3" = 1"

Through Wainscot

Single Door

Sliding Door

Through Panel Back

Door Transom

Base & Trim Principal Rooms

Box for Blinds

Picture Mould

THE HAYES'
SKYLIGHTS

LOUVRE AND OTHER VENTILATORS.

Architectural and Sanitary Specialties.

PERFORATED SHEET METALS.

GEORGE HAYES,

Nos. 71 & 73 EIGHTH AVENUE,

NEW YORK.

(TELEPHONE CALL, 85—21st STREET.)

SKYLIGHT LITIGATION.

71 8TH AVENUE, NEW YORK, March 3d, 1882.

The Profession and Trade will be pleased to learn that his honor, Judge BLATCHFORD, has again rendered a decision in y favor —after a very severe and well contested trial—giving, in his written decision, a most conclusive opinion.

The record of the United States Circuit Court for the Southern District of New York now stands:

| HAYES vs. ICKSON & GIBSON. | "The usual decree for Plaintiff with costs." SAML. BLATCHFORD, *Circuit Judge.* Nov. 26th, 1880. | SETON vs. HAYES. | "This suit be and the same hereby is discontinued with costs to the defendant to be taxed by the Clerk." SAML. BLATCHFORD, Nov. 15th, 1881. *Circuit Judge.* (This suit was predicated upon the alleged infringement of the "Weston Patent.") | HAYES vs. BORKEL. | "The usual decree for Plaintiff with costs." SAML. BLATCHFORD, *Circuit Judge.* March 3d, 1882. |

The law determines as infringers, all who Make, Use, Vend, or Sell, or those having in their possession for Sale or Use, y article upon which a Valid Patent has been obtained. (Vide United States Statutes, Sec. 4,884, and Sec. 4,919.) And in der to get back some of the vast outlay in obtaining my rights, I shall elect to collect from the Owners of buildings as Users, l not from the Makers, who, as a rule, are impecunious and irresponsible.

I promise that, notwithstanding the successful termination of the contest, as here recorded, I do not propose to take any lue advantage, or to exact from the public exorbitant prices, but shall continue to give nothing but first-class work at a fair ce, and thus sustain the reputation heretofore accorded me. Respectfully yours,

GEORGE HAYES.

☞ It must now be understood that the Court has decided as infringements, all Metallic Skylights having in combination, gutters in the and cross gutters, whether located at the ridge, Base, Intermediate or elsewhere. And also with Ridge Ventilators, and many other details, r or all of which is absolutely necessary for a complete and perfect skylight. And that all subsequent patents are void in this regard. G. H

 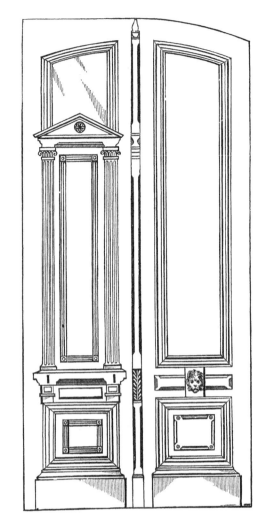

C. B. KEOGH & CO.,

MANUFACTURERS OF

DOORS, SASHES AND BLINDS,

PINE OR HARD WOOD.

SPECIAL ATTENTION GIVEN TO

ALL KINDS OF **CABINET TRIM,** IN ALL THE

FANCY WOODS.

---

203 & 205 CANAL STREET,

→✳NEW YORK.✳←

C. B. KEOGH.   H. C. McKAY.   H. C. SMITH

A · ROYAL · PORCELAIN · BATH

AS · FITTED · UP · IN · WAREROOMS · OF · HENRY · C · MEYER · & · CO.

OTTO F. FALCK,

Ecclesiastical & Domestic Glass Stainin

HALL, LIBRARY & STAIR-CASE WINDOWS,

—AND—

Memorial Windows for Churches.

34 EAST HOUSTON STREET,

Two blocks east of Broadway,   NEW YOR

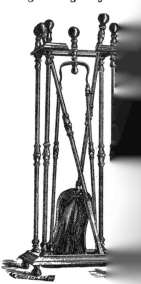

✦FINE ARTS✦

HAT we are rapidly developing into an art-loving people goes without saying. On all sides evidence is accumulating of this fact. It can be seen in the importation of pictures of the very highest grade, and the largely-increasing attendance at art sales and annual exhibitions. It can be seen in the growing knowledge of many arts and their accessories with which we were unfamiliar a few years ago. It can be seen in dress and in furniture and house decoration, until it would seem that the ingenuity of man had been taxed to its utmost to produce new and effective designs in the latter goods to please the eye. It is but a few years ago that hair-cloth and rep-covered furniture were considered quite in keeping with most persons of wealth. Gradually satin coverings took their place, carpets had to be in keeping, and the acme of house adornment was to be able to have a satin-finished paper on the wall; ceiling decoration was confined to a few shades prepared by that man of genius, the kalsominer. The times have veritably changed, and to-day household decoration is as great a study and as high an art as the most finished work of a Diaz, Corot, or Meissonier. The labor and genius employed may not command so high a remuneration as one of the great artists would demand for similar time employed; but that it does require high order of talent is beyond question, and the verification of this needs only a visit to the establishment of **Messrs. Fr. Beck & Co.**, manufacturers of wall papers, corner of Seventh Avenue and Twenty-ninth Street, to witness its convincing proof. As the tastes of the people have improved, so has this firm kept pace with the demand; in fact, it has, to a great extent, led the taste and fostered the desire for a higher education in house decoration. All that improved machinery could do has been employed by them, the best talent attainable has been secured, and the most commodious factory and warerooms built for their business and customers. Their latest designs are simply marvels of wall and ceiling decoration,— tapestry and velvets, the latter not an imitation, but a *real velvet*, in most exquisite figures and shades, attached to a paper back, and hung with as much facility as ordinary wall paper. They have also succeeded in reproducing the effects of the old Venetian or Dutch leathers in exceedingly odd designs, harmonizing where the surrounding accessories are dark. Another novelty is the reproduction of patterns in imitation of oxidized metals, steel, iron, bronze and brass, appearing at a little distance to be the heavy metals they but represent. It is marvelous how real they seem. With their unexcelled facilities they can reproduce any pattern made abroad, and often at half the price asked for imported goods. Our galleries are daily thronged by those interested in art and its advancement, but a greater and far more interesting study can be seen at **Messrs. Beck & Co.'s** warerooms, where courteous attendants are always glad to show visitors through their factory and explain what they are doing to advance the taste for house decoration.—*New York Evening Express.*

Furniture, Interior Decorations, &c.

While we always have in our Warerooms, a well assorted and very large Stock of

RICH FURNITURE

We are also prepared to furnish DESIGNS and ESTIMATES

FOR

ORDERED WORK—RICH OR PLAIN

Which with our large facilities we can execute promptly, and in the very best manner.

DOREMUS & CORBETT,

Warerooms: 148, 150, 152 and 154 West 23d Street, - - NEW YORK